Camp Summer Read

Camp Summer Read

How to Create Your Own Summer Reading Camp

C. Kay Gooch and Charlotte Massey

LIBRARIES UNLIMITED

AN IMPRINT OF ABC-CLIO, LLC
Santa Barbara, California • Denver, Colorado • Oxford, England

The authors thank Jo Kretzler for
providing the illustrations for this book.

Library of Congress Cataloging-in-Publication Data

Gooch, C. Kay.
    Camp summer read : how to create your own summer reading camp / C. Kay
Gooch and Charlotte Massey.
       p. cm
    Includes bibliographical references and index.
    ISBN 978-1-59884-447-4 (acid-free paper) 1. Children's
libraries—Activity programs—United States. 2. School
libraries—Activity programs—United States. 3. Summer reading
programs—United States. 4. Children—Books and reading—United States.
I. Massey, Charlotte, 1968– II. Title.
Z718.3.G66 2011
027.62'5—dc22   2010041100

ISBN: 978-1-59884-447-4
EISBN: 978-1-59884-448-1

15 14 13 12 11   1 2 3 4 5

This book is also available on the World Wide Web as an eBook.
Visit www.abc-clio.com for details.

Libraries Unlimited
An Imprint of ABC-CLIO, LLC

ABC-CLIO, LLC
130 Cremona Drive, P.O. Box 1911
Santa Barbara, California 93116-1911

This book is printed on acid-free paper ∞
Manufactured in the United States of America

Contents

Introduction

Welcome to Camp Summer Read! It's a great way to keep everyone reading over the summer. The children will relate to and experience books in a fun and creative way. They will remember *One Potato, Two Potato* by Cynthia DeFelice after participating in the potato races!

They will remember *Outside and Inside Mummies* by Sandra Markle after dressing up and dancing to Steve Martin's "King Tut" and wrapping each other up like a mummy! We are here to tell you how to do it all! So go ahead—grab a book, do some planning, and have fun reading this summer. We'll show you how easy and fun it can be.

Benefits of Reading Aloud

Reading aloud is an important, worthwhile activity. When we read aloud to children, we share ourselves, our background experiences, and our love of literature. More specifically, we share a book, everything found in it, and more, including excitement, emotion, characters, and fun. Children learn that reading is enjoyable. For example, after reading *The SOS Files* by Betsy Byars, we all shared times when we had an emergency experience. Many of the children shared stories about being lost in a mall or going to the emergency room for stitches. Having adults listen to their fears and worries as well as their exciting experiences gives credibility to their feelings. As we share our experiences, children learn they are not the only ones with these emotions. We can all be connected with each other as well as to the words in the book. It will no longer be just a story on the page; it becomes something we could feel and even see as we share our scars.

This is a great way to connect with children in a relaxed and comfortable setting and to share our life experiences with them. The more you can share these experiences, the more background knowledge children can come away with to connect to other stories. Reading aloud also enriches oral language development and broadens conceptual backgrounds. It models for children what reading sounds like. When children hear adults read with expression and emotion, they know the sound of reading and can mimic and learn from the modeled behavior.

Who We Are

We are two elementary school librarians from the Austin, Texas area who met on the first day of orientation at the School of Library and Information Science at the University of Texas at Austin. After that first day, we spent the next year and a half taking all our classes together. Then we got our first library jobs together (at different schools), had babies, and graduated our children from high school. We have been through thick and thin together! Part of our friendship has been that we have the same basic philosophy about being elementary school librarians: We want our students to become good readers, lifelong learners, and lovers of books, and we think they should have fun throughout the process!

How We Started

We have spent our ten years as school librarians bouncing ideas off each other and trying to make our curriculums the best they can be. We collaborate on topics, holidays, grade levels, authors, library arrangement, job opportunities, and the kitchen sink. At the Texas Library Association Conference several years ago, we learned that many librarians promoted the Texas Bluebonnet Award list in a variety of ways. They were doing these activities during their free time—for free! We loved the ideas but wanted to make extra money doing it. We realized that at our schools, many families sent their children to summer camps. Why couldn't we create a camp to help the parents with the summer care *and* help the students get a jump-start on our state reading program? We look forward to each new list and a summer of fun and reading.

We set out our goals to create a camp where the students would end the experience with an accomplished goal, having been exposed to different books on our state list and having had a great time doing it. It took us a couple of years to come up with the right formula. We know we have been successful because the campers return year after year, and parents plan their children's summer activities around when *we* have *our* camp! We are writing this book so you can create your own camp without having to go through the agony of two years of trial and error to get it right. We will tell you what we have done—the good, the bad and the really ugly—so that you can jump in and take off.

The Format

This book is designed to help you make the right decisions for your camp so that it fits your style. We will tell you about how we do our camp.

HOW WE DO IT HOW WE DO IT

Then we will list questions

that you need to consider to make sure your camp will work for you. We hope this will help you jump-start your camp with the knowledge of a working formula. We spent a lot of time worrying about and guessing how to do things and wondering if it would work. We will take that worrying and guessing out of the equation for you, so that you can have a successful experience.

Our camp is designed as an enrichment summer activity for a public elementary school, but many of our ideas can easily be adopted for a children's librarian at a public library. Many settings are possible for reading camps. Although we have to follow the guidelines of our schools and we want our purpose fulfilled, we realize not everyone has the same goals and requirements. Throughout this book, we give you suggestions to adapt your camp to meet your needs. We also include modifications

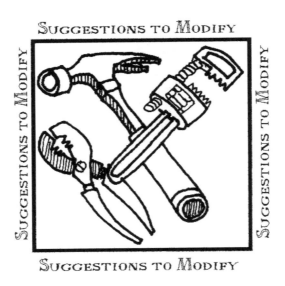

that will further help you customize your camp to your audience.

Our camp is flexible and, above all, it's FUN!

Chapter 1

Getting Started

Summer Camp

Throughout this book, the one thing you will hear us harp on over and over about our reading camp is that it must be **FUN!** It takes place during summer, and we have to make sure the campers are learning something—but the learning component has to be disguised as fun. We want to make sure the students have a good day at camp so that they want to come back the next day, and even the next year.

We plan our camp as a half-day camp, but we offer some suggestions on doing full-day camps, too. Our goal is to complete six books from our reading list—all nominees for the Texas Bluebonnet Award—by the end of the camp week. This way, when school starts, students have already met the minimum reading requirement to vote on books for the annual award. Your state may require that a different number of books be read for students to be able to vote, or you may choose a list unrelated to an award. Regardless, after completing several books during summer camp, campers can achieve higher levels and read more difficult books once school starts.

Preparing for your camp means many decisions need to be made beyond the choice of your theme or your books, which we discuss in a later chapter. You need to decide how long you will hold your camp, how many camps you can accommodate over the summer, how to register your campers, where you will hold the camp, and whether you will charge students to attend. Accounting for funds is another challenge to solve before your first campers arrive.

Length of Camp

Early on you will need to decide exactly how long you wish to offer your camp. This will make a difference in how many children you can accommodate for this summer event. Our camp is held for a half day for one week. We have two sessions, one from 9 AM to noon and another session from 1 to 4 PM. This gives us plenty of time to complete all the activities planned for the day. Each day, we read the book of the day, introduce a couple of the other books on our list, enjoy two activities, have snack time, and conclude the day by reading one or two chapters from one of the shorter chapter books on the list. We try to be able to complete one chapter book by the end of the week, in addition to the "books of the day."

You may want to consider whether to do a half-day or full-day camp. If you're doing a full-day camp, you need to consider several things. How will you handle lunch? Will you provide it, or will the campers bring their own? You will need to have more books and activities. It may be helpful to use books with a common theme. If you choose not to, then you need to decide how to handle the transitions between books. You may want to build in a rest time for full-day camps. This can be in conjunction with lunch. During this time, you could read aloud from a chapter book, or the campers could have a free reading time. If your camp is full day, you need to consider the beginning and ending times for your camp. Will it coincide with the parents' workday to take the place of day care?

Another thing you must decide is just how many camps you can offer during the summer and when to offer them. These decisions are affected by when and where to hold the camp.

How Many Camps?

We usually offer four camp sessions. We had to add a session at one of the schools one year because our waiting list was so long. We try to limit our camps to twenty students. If there are special cases, sometimes we may add one or two campers over that. When deciding how many camps to hold, we think about how many weeks we are willing to give up during the summer break. We both like to take a trip or two during the summer, so we have to make sure we have time for that and ample time off to relax before we return to work for the school year. We also consider our stamina. Doing two 3-hour camps in one day is a very long, tiring day. Also, we have to get approval from our campuses for the number of weeks we are going to be in session.

When to Hold the Camps

We have done our camps at different times during the summer. One year it was early in the summer, another year it was in the middle, and another it was at the very end of summer. No time is ideal; it just depends on what is happening in your schedule. Regardless of when we have the camp, we have been able to fill most of our sessions. We check with other school camps to see what their schedules are so we don't overlap. We try to check in with other activities, such as the swim teams, junior drill team camps, or all-star little league schedules as well.

The year we held camp close to the end of summer, the parents were happy because they had exhausted all the other camps for their children to attend. Having it at the end of summer gave us a lot of time to plan, but it also ran right up to the end of summer and didn't leave much time to recover before the beginning of school. The summer we held our camp at the beginning of summer, we worked really hard to have it ready, but then the rest of summer was ours to do other things.

Where to Hold the Camps

We have been able to hold our camps in our own libraries. This is a familiar place to both our students and us, and it is geographically close to most of their homes. If you can do this, be prepared to pay a fee for use of the facility. Your principal will need to assign custodial help to your library and the nearby restrooms because this would not normally be an assignment during the summer.

You may not be able to hold your camp in your own school library. You may need to ask someone in your community parks and recreation department for a suggestion or a local church or other organization with a meeting room. They will be able to tell you about the cost for use of the facility, if a kitchen is available to prepare or refrigerate snacks, the configuration of any room available for your use (tables and chairs at an appropriate size, a cozy area for reading to children, comfortable spots for children to sit and read), and what is available if you want to go outside for a short time.

One of the challenges you may find in selecting a site, even your own library, is having computers available for part of your programming. If you do not have computers, you may need to substitute a flip chart in place of the wiki we use to share information every day.

Registration

We try to have our dates in place by February because that is when the parents and the students start asking us for our camp information. Our registration flyers go out around the first of March. By spring break, most of the parents are scheduling what their children will be doing for the summer, and we want to make sure we are at the top of their lists. We actually do have some parents who schedule their other activities around our camp!

Our registration form is clear, to the point, simple, and easy to follow (see Appendix A). We have our form printed on bright paper. When picking the color of paper for the registration form, think about having it go with the theme of your camp (ours is bright blue in honor of the Bluebonnet Award), and make sure it is a color that you can read easily, both for the parents who fill it out, and for you when you'll be reading the completed forms. Bright red seems like a good idea in the beginning, but it is difficult to read as a copy and nearly impossible to read when a child has filled it out in pencil! We have all the important information included, such as allergy information, special needs, medical issues, and so on. Our last line on the send-back portion asks for any information we might need to know about the child. We are asking directly for information about concerns such as food allergies or attention-deficit disorder. We don't want any surprises, such as "We decided to not give Eddie his meds for the summer!" As discussed in Chapter 5, we also make it very clear that our snacks may not be nutritious but are an extension the featured books. We ask for a nonrefundable deposit upfront, with the remainder due before school is out for the summer.

One of our schools has a weekly take-home folder that includes all information for parents, but the other school does not. So we make sure that parents at both schools are aware that the camp flyer is out. We have its distribution announced on the school listserv so parents will know to look for the flyers. We make sure we talk about it in all our classes during library times. We also make sure that any key parent groups talk about our camp to their friends. We encourage children to bring their friends from other schools, and we encourage those children to bring another friend from their school.

Money

Payment can be such a touchy subject. Please remember, we are not accountants, and we do what we know to be true and honest. If you have any questions, please consult your local tax expert. The one thing to keep in mind is this is not "free money," as some would like to believe. It is income and needs to be treated that way.

What to Charge, or Should We Charge?

The answer to this question may come from what the real purpose is for presenting your camp. If you are doing it to earn extra income, you obviously have to charge. If you are doing it as an incentive for students to read during the summer and someone else is funding it, you don't have to charge. If you are doing the camp as a fundraiser for your library, you charge accordingly. If you are doing it as a public service out of a public library, you may want to charge a small fee to cover your costs.

One thing you might want to consider is that if you start your camp for free, you may never be able to charge for it later. You can always change the charge for your camp, either raising or lowering the fee, but rarely can you start charging for something you have done for free in the past. We have raised our price once. The other camps at our school were changing the price of their camps, so we went with the consensus group.

When determining the charge for your camp, be sure to consider your population. One of our schools is in a middle-class neighborhood, the other school is not. We may do exactly the same camp at both schools, but at the school with a lower socioeconomic level, we do not charge as much. We still have to cover our expenses, but we may not be able to make as much for our efforts. When considering this, you have to go back to your basic reason for offering the camp. It can't be all about the money. We all know that if that were the case, this is not necessarily the profession we would have chosen in the first place.

Once you have decided the purpose for holding your camp, you need to decide whether you are going to charge for it and how much. The purpose of our camp is to earn extra income for us; it is our summer job. We originally based our camp fee on what other summer camps charged. We need to make enough to make it worth giving up three or four weeks during the summer. We make sure we charge enough to cover any building use fee that is incurred as well as supplies and snacks. We try to keep the supply and snack expenditure to about $10–$15 per child for the week. Each time we plan an activity, we figure in its cost. The same is done for each snack.

If you are doing this as a fundraiser you need to set your fee according to the purpose of your fundraiser. If you are supplementing your library budget for the purchase of new shelving or another project, make sure your gross covers that objective.

If you are doing the camp as a nonprofit endeavor, you need to be sure you have the funding to cover activities and snacks. Whether this comes from a grant, local funds, or your own pocket, you need to make sure you consider the source.

How Do You Do Your Accounting?

We have done our accounting two ways. We designate one of us to be the money handler. This is a big job, but it is better if money is only going through one set of hands at a time. The really big question is whether to do it through a personal banking account or run it through the school, which we now discuss in turn.

Through the school account: If you are going to fund all the money through your school, you have to abide by all the rules and regulations of its accounting department. You will have to pay yourself at a rate that is set by your school. You will have your taxes taken out by your district, as well as social security and retirement. Of course, you are going to want to get every penny out of the paid tuition, so this can be a really tricky thing. You can only pay yourself x number of hours a day, x number of days a week. These regulations are usually set by the school district. What we did is pay ourselves for planning time, actual camp time, and a little clean-up time. When you account for the money this way, your actual check for camp will not be as large because of all the deductions. It will also not be on your time schedule, it will be on the district's schedule. You also need to know that it will be in your paycheck as salary, so it will affect your retirement numbers. All snacks and crafts need to be purchased outright and then are reimbursed through the school account. As always, make sure you talk to the bookkeeper at your school who will be handling the money. Make sure that person knows what he or she is doing.

Through a personal account: When we ran the camp finances through a personal account, the first thing we did was set up a separate account especially for camp. We did not even try to run this through one of our own personal accounts. The account is used only for camp. We make sure we have a checkbook and a debit card for all our expenses. You have to make sure you keep every receipt and keep good records. We make sure we keep copies of all checks written to us and make sure we give everyone a receipt (see Appendix A). We keep a spreadsheet of all our expenses, such as snacks and supplies for activities. When tax season comes around, we take it all to our tax preparers, and they put it in with our taxes. Although this method may seem like you are earning more money in the beginning, you will be receiving funds from which no income tax has been deducted, and you will be paying taxes on it as income along with your other earnings at tax time.

Some parents will deduct your camp as child care. If you are wary of giving your social security number out for their records, you will need to consult your local tax consultant.

The following questions will help you make your decisions as you plan your camp.

When deciding the length of your camp, consider the following questions:

- Do you want to do half-day camps or full-day camps?

- If you are doing full-day camps:

    - What will you do about lunch?

    - Will you need more activities?

    - Will you try to cover more than one book each day?

    - Will you have free reading time to fill some of the extra time?

    - Will you be taking the place of day care for some of the students?

    - What will your hours be?

When deciding how many camp sessions to hold, consider the following questions:

- How many students will you have?

- How many weeks are you willing to offer the camps?

- How many weeks is your campus going to allow you to have camp?

- How many camps can you fill?

- At what point are you willing to add another session?

- At what point are you willing to combine sessions if there aren't enough campers?

- Will you physically and emotionally be able to endure numerous sessions of camp?

When deciding where to hold your camp, consider the following questions:

- Will your school library be available for your use during the summer?

- If it is not available, what are your other options?

- What will it cost to use the facility?

- Will a different facility have the spaces you need to hold your camp?

When deciding what to charge for your camp, consider the following questions:

- What is the purpose of the camp?

- Is this a fundraiser for school?

- Is the camp intended to earn additional income for you, separate from your regular job?

- Is the camp a community activity that anyone is welcome to attend without charge?

- What are the activities going to cost?

- What will snacks cost?

Now that you've considered some of the organizational aspects of running a reading camp, we'll look at book selection in the next chapter.

Chapter 2

Book Selection

How We Do It How We Do It

As Texas educators, we find it easy to center our camp around the Texas Bluebonnet Award (TBA) list, which are the books nominated for the state's children's choice book award. The TBA list is published every November and has plenty of read-aloud picture books, and the camp helps us promote the Bluebonnet programs we hold in our libraries. However, you can use any book list you want, and you will find many from which to choose. When choosing your books, be sure to select books with pictures that you can read aloud in about ten to twenty minutes. As noted in the previous chapter, you can also choose a shorter chapter book that can be completed in one week. We read one to two chapters to finish up each day. To ensure repeat campers, you will want to choose different books each year.

If you follow our plan and you live in Texas, you can follow our lead. Obviously, not all our readers will live in Texas, so many of you will want to find out more about your own state's reading list(s). It may be that a list is compiled through the joint effort of several associations whose members develop the list, and the grade levels for student voting will vary. We have found, however, that using a state reading list is helpful because it has applications even after our camp has concluded and the school year has begun.

Each November, the Texas Library Association (TLA) publishes a reading list nominating books for the TBA, the premier children's choice book award for Texas. This list features twenty books and includes a variety of picture books, early chapter books, and more advanced chapter books. The list is intended for grades 3 through 6. We use this list as a motivational reading incentive program in both of our schools. It is readily available on the TLA website (www.txla. org). The TBA Committee provides helpful annotations of the books, as well as other useful things, such as reader's theater scripts, booktalks, and more.

Because we use the current TBA list each year, we need to revise our camp annually. We have many repeat campers each year, so our offering must be fresh and, in addition, it must go with our current year's curriculum. Another advantage of using our state's reading list is that if a book has been chosen for the TBA list, it is readily available, and it is one we are going to purchase for our libraries.

When the list is announced in November, we get copies of the books as quickly as we can. We organize the books according to their length. We look over the books that can be read in one sitting. Once we have determined their length, we look at the theme of the books and decide which ones have the best potential for activities. We like to have diverse activities for camp week in terms of topics as well as fun and educational activities.

For a weeklong, half-day camp, we use one picture book per day. If your camp is a full-day camp, then you may want to use several books each day, organized around a single daily theme. We always keep in mind that the topic has to be something that will interest the campers. We can twist and stretch a subject that we want to teach so the children get hooked on a given topic. We also pick one shorter chapter book that can be read each day as we wrap up. We can usually finish one short chapter book, and sometimes even start another.

Because we use the TBA list for our library reading incentive program, we like to introduce all the books on the list, even those we don't read at camp. We do this by taking time at the beginning of each day to booktalk several titles on the list.

Appendix B provides a sampling of books we have used for Camp Summer Read, with a brief synopsis of each.

When picking a list to use for your camp, ask the following questions:

- How many books can I include in one week?

- Is there a children's book award in my state to guide the selection process?

- Do I want to change my camp every year to match a new book list?

- Is there a list in my area that may be used for reading incentive?

- Is there a reading incentive program at my library that I can use to help create my camp reading list?

- Will the students' accomplishments in camp count toward the incentive I run during the school year?

Lists to Help Create Your Camp Summer Read

When using a list created by an organization that selects a new list annually, you can use past years' lists as well as the current one. Some examples of annual lists are:

- Luminarias (Spanish/English)

- Mockingbird (Abilene, Texas)

- Texas Bluebonnet Award

- 2X2 (Texas Library Association)

- Children's Choice K–2 (CBC)

Children's Choice and Favorite Books Lists by State

Here we provide the name of each state's book award list and the grade levels to which the awards apply. This information is available on state websites, but URLs change so rapidly that we chose not to provide them. Check your state library association's website first, or type the name of the award into an Internet search engine. Note that many states have two or more library associations (e.g., the California Library Association and the California School Library Association; the Pennsylvania Library Association and the Pennsylvania School Librarians Association), and they may be joint sponsors of the children's choice contest. However, if you don't find any information on one association's website, please look at the alternate.

State and Book List (Target Grades)

Alabama—Camellia Award (K–1) (2–3) (4–6)

Alaska—Battle of the Books (3–4) (5–6)

Arizona—Grand Canyon Reader Award (Picture) (Intermediate)

Arkansas—Charlie May Simon Children's Book Award (4–6)

Arkansas—Arkansas Diamond Primary Book Award (K–3)

California—California Young Reader Medal (Primary) (Intermediate)

Colorado—Colorado Children's Book Award (Picture) (Junior)

Colorado—Blue Spruce Award (YA)

Connecticut—Nutmeg Book Award (4–8)

Delaware—Blue Hen Book Award

Delaware—Delaware Diamonds Booklist (K–12)

Florida—Florida Children's Book Award (Pre-K–2)

Florida—Sunshine State Young Readers Award (3–8)

Georgia—Georgia Children's Book Award, Picture Storybook (K–4)

Georgia—Georgia Children's Book Award, Book (4–8)

Georgia—Georgia Peach Book Award for Teen Readers (9–12)

Illinois—The Monarch Award (K–3)

Illinois—Rebecca Caudill Young Reader's Book Award (4–8)

Indiana—Indiana Read Aloud Books—Too Good to Miss (K–12)

Indiana—Young Hoosier Book Awards (K–8)

Iowa—The Goldfinch Award (Pre-K–3)

Iowa—Iowa Children's Choice Award (4–8)

Kansas—William Allen White Children's Book Awards (3–5) (6–8)

Kansas—Bill Martin Jr. Picture Book Award

Kentucky—The Bluegrass Award (K–2) (3–5) (6–8) (9–12)

Louisiana—Louisiana Young Readers' Choice Award (3–5) (6–8)

Maine—Maine Student Book Award (4–8)

Maryland—Maryland Black-Eyed Susan Book Award (Picture) (4–6) (6–9)

Maryland—Maryland Blue Crab Young Reader Award

Massachusetts—Massachusetts Children's Book Award (4–6)

Michigan—MRA Great Lakes Great Books

Minnesota—Maud Hart Lovelace Book Award (3–5) (6–8)

Missouri—Building Block Award (Pre-K–2)

Missouri—Mark Twain Award (4–6)

Missouri—Show Me Readers Award (1 –3)

Montana—Treasure State Award (K–3)

Nebraska—Golden Sower Award (Primary) (Intermediate)

Nevada—Nevada Young Readers' Award (Picture) (Young Readers)

New Hampshire—Ladybug Picture Book Award (Pre–K–3)

New Jersey—Garden State Book Awards

New Mexico—Land of Enchantment Book Award (K–9)

New York—Charlotte Award

New York—3 Apples Book Award (Pre-K–2) (3–6)

North Carolina—North Carolina Children's Book Award (Picture) (Junior)

North Dakota—Flicker Tale Children's Book Award

Ohio—The Buckeye Children's Book Award

Oklahoma—Sequoyah Book Award (3–5) (6–8)

Pacific Northwest—Young Readers' Choice Award (4–6)

Oregon—Beverly Cleary Children's Choice Award (2–3)

Oregon—Patricia Gallagher Picture Book Award

Pennsylvania—Keystone to Reading Book Award (Primary) (Intermediate)

Pennsylvania—The Pennsylvania Young Reader's Choice Award (K–3) (3–6)

Rhode Island—Rhode Island Children's Book Award (3–6)

South Carolina—South Carolina Book Award (Picture) (Children's)

South Dakota—SD Children's Book Award—Prairie Bud (K–2)

South Dakota—SD Children's Book Award—Prairie Pasque (3–5)

Tennessee—Volunteer State Book Award (K–3) (4–6)

Texas—Texas Bluebonnet Award (3–6)

Texas—2X2 Reading List (Pre-K–2)

Utah—Beehive Award (Picture) (Children's Poetry)

Vermont—Red Clover Award (K–4)

Virginia—Virginia Readers' Choice (K–3) (3–5)

Washington—Washington Children's Choice Picture Book Award (K–3)

Washington—Sasquatch Reading Award (3–6)

West Virginia—Moonbeam Children's Book Award (Many Levels)

Wisconsin—The Golden Archer Award (Primary) (Intermediate)

Wyoming—Buckaroo Book Award (K–3)

Wyoming—Indian Paintbrush Book Award (4–6)

You can try choosing books based on a theme:

- Fairy tales

- Scary stories

- Holidays

- Summer/Seasons

- Caldecott Award-Winning Books

- Biographies/Famous people

- Tall tales

- Myths (Greek, Roman, etc.)

- Ocean/Beach

- Families

- America

- Multicultural

- Cookbooks

You might like to focus on the curricular areas:

- Math books

- Science books

- History books

- Writing

You could focus on favorite authors:

- Eric Carle

- Tomie dePaola

- Jan Brett

- Cynthia Rylant

- Lois Ehlert

- Audrey Wood

- Janet Stevens and Susan Stevens Crummel

There are also some great Internet links to help with lists and books to find to use at your camp:

- Carol Hurst's Children's Literature Site—www.carolhurst.com/index.html

- Peggy Sharp—www.peggysharp.com

- Bookhive—www.bookhive.org

- Teachers First—www.teachersfirst.com/100books.cfm

- Children's Book Council—www.cbcbooks.org/readinglists

- New York Times Bestsellers/Children's Books—www.nytimes.com

- Oprah's Kids' Reading Lists—www.oprah.com/packages/kid-reading-lists.html

- About.com—childrensbooks.about.com

Here is a checklist to help with your book selection:

- Pick your favorite books, independent of a list.

- Design your camp around one grade level instead of mixing ages: one week for third grade, one week for fourth grade, and so on.

- Let the children come up with the list of books or authors they want to study.

- Use the summer reading theme that your local public library is sponsoring.

- Pick a theme that children are always interested in, such as, dogs, safari, or circuses, and develop the whole camp around that theme.

Because we use the Texas Bluebonnet Award list for our program, we coordinate with our local public librarians. We let them know what we're doing, and they can coordinate and promote their own activities during our camp. We encourage our campers to go to the public library and look for books from our list or that extend our list. It is a good idea to talk to your public librarian regardless of which titles you decide to use. This can be helpful in your planning.

Once you have selected your books, you can begin to choose the activities to accompany your choices. This process is covered in the next chapter.

Chapter 3

Activities

You can include many types of activities in your summer camp. We try to create ones that are fun, easy to manage, and inexpensive. We like the campers to have some products from the activities that can be taken home at the end of camp week. We also look for activities that are educational without seeming like schoolwork. Crafts, games, experiments, research, and information sharing activities have all worked well for us. This chapter provides many examples of activities from which to choose. Appendix C provides more information about planning activities around the books you choose, using titles we've used very successfully at Camp Summer Read.

In creating our activities, we utilize a variety of resources.

- Our experience as classroom teachers and librarians is invaluable. We use activities we have done at school over the years, as well as what we have seen other educators do successfully.

- We peruse the Internet for all kinds of activities. We usually start with a simple search with key words, such as "children's activities dogs."

- We have used purchased activities from online craft stores. We try not to purchase too many premade activities, but sometimes you find just that perfect "outer-space necklace" that you can't resist!

- We have made up things just because they sounded good.

- We have gotten many ideas from online fee-based educational resource sites. These are plentiful, and usually the fee is nominal. This is a great resource for word searches, diagrams, maps, question activities, and so much more.

Whatever activity you decide to do, it is a good idea to try it out well before the week of camp. Finding out the night before, for example, that the size of dog biscuit you have purchased is not going to work for your activity is a nightmare in the making!

Activity for Beginning of Day

Each camper is given a legal-sized manila folder on the first day of camp. This folder is theirs for the week, and at the end of camp, it goes home with them with all of their completed activities inside. They are free to color and draw all over the folder to make it special to them.

Every day when the campers come in, they find a packet of activities that goes along with the theme of the day. This packet includes activities such as crossword puzzles, acrostic poems, word finds, coloring pages, definition matching activities, reading materials about the topic of the day, or anything else we can come up with. We also include an information page about the book we are reading that day. This page has a picture of the cover of the book, the title and author, and a brief synopsis. We also include other books the campers might read if they like this selection. The objective of the folder is for the campers to have something to keep them busy while everyone else is arriving at camp (unlike the school year, this is *summer* camp, and not everyone is going to run on a tight schedule). The campers also use the folders to work on during the camp day when they have finished an activity and are waiting for the others to complete theirs. Campers often pull out their folders while having snacks and work on things together. Appendix D provides a selection of Internet resources to help choose activities for your camp, and Appendix E is a sample of what a packet based on a dog theme might include.

Wiki

For each day, we create a wiki that has readily available information about the topic of the day. It is a good way to organize any relevant websites, online games, or activities. Sometimes we use these as part of our activity, but it is also helpful during downtime like snack time or if an activity finishes early. The campers like to use each wiki to explore and extend. This provides another way to look at the subject when campers are settling in for the day or have free time between activities.

For example, when we read the book *Pale Male: Citizen Hawk of New York City* by Janet Schulman, we included the following information and links on a wiki:

- Title and author of the book

- Summary of the book

- Birdsong link—an interesting, award-winning site where users can click on a picture of a bird to hear its song

- Everything birds link—a collection of information that included tons of sites, lesson plans, activities, projects, and anything you might want to know about birds

- Hummingbirds—Kristine O'Connell's link provides information on her hummingbird poetry book

- The Legend of Pale Male link—the site of a documentary film on the story of Pale Male. We watched clips from the documentary, including the picketing that happened outside the hotel. It verified the information in the book perfectly!

- Rate the Bluebonnet Book site—because we use our state award list, we always put a link to a site where campers can rate the book after they read it.

On our *Help Me, Mr. Mutt: Expert Answers for Dogs with People Problems* by Janet Stevens and Susan Stevens Crummel wiki, we also included some great game sites, one from Animal Planet's web page and one from PBS Kid's web page. We also included a link to the author's website. If the author and illustrator have sites, we include those on our wiki as well.

Campers are free to go to any wiki we have introduced. We have each wiki bookmarked on the browsers of each computer to make it easy for the campers to find. We are sure to put the wiki address on the cover of each activity packet as well so campers can continue to access the information from home.

Choosing Activities

We choose our activities by considering the amount of time and expense they will take, as well as whether campers will find them fun to do. Of course, we also need to know what's featured in the book.

So first, we read the book thoroughly! This means reading the foreword, the text, and the author's note at the end. It also means looking at the endpapers, the cover design, illustrations, the front and back flaps, the CIP information, and any other supporting materials in the book. These are parts of the book that students often skip, and we want to make sure they understand their importance. We expect the students to read the entire book, and so we make sure we read it all the way through as well. Many times, the author and illustrator biographies go along with the book's theme or plot and reveal the authors' personalities to the campers. It is nice for the campers to relate to the authors and illustrators and see that they are real people. Sometimes we create activities that tie in the parts of the book that are supporting materials.

In one instance, we were reading *The Luck of the Loch Ness Monster: A Tale of Picky Eating* by Alice Flaherty. The book talks about a picky eater who throws her oatmeal overboard. Doing activities with the Loch Ness monster and snacks with oatmeal were pretty obvious choices, but we took it a step further when we discovered on the back flap that the author only ate peanut butter and jelly sandwiches on white bread when she was a girl. We then made a chart about picky eaters and foods they enjoy.

Clearly, when we choose an activity, it has to tie in with the book. If the book is about dogs, we choose two activities that have to do with dogs. Sometimes a book has more than one theme. One activity might be a craft project, such as making a dog puppet, and the other might be a story written as a poem. Some days we do two fun activities, and some days we do one fun activity and one academic activity. For example, when we used the book *Help Me Mr. Mutt!: Expert Answers for Dogs with People Problems* by Janet Stevens and Susan Stevens Crummel, in addition to a dog craft activity, we had the campers write letters to a friend or relative. The campers made their own personalized stationery to write their letters. They had to bring an address of someone to write to, address a real envelope, and use a real stamp, not just send a note by e-mail. The excitement came when they got calls from a grandmother in Colorado or a cousin in California saying that they had received a real letter from the camper.

When choosing an activity for a book, it is important to keep in mind the amount of time it will take to complete it. The hours of your camp may dictate which and how many activities you can accomplish. Keep in mind that this is summer camp, and the campers have very short attention spans. Completing an activity in one sitting is imperative. If you do an activity that takes two "activity sessions," keep in mind where you will leave off and where you will pick it up when you return to it. The campers need to be excited about coming back to complete the activity, whether it is an hour or two later or the next day. If the activity is going to take a couple of days to complete, make sure you schedule the book early in the week. When we read *George Crum and the Saratoga Chip* by Gaylia Taylor, we did an activity in which we grew rye grass seeds in a "potato head." This activity included making a potato head out of a real potato with googly eyes, beads, yarn, and pipe-cleaner mouths. We hollowed out the top of the head, filled it with potting soil and rye grass seed, watered them every morning, and by the end of the week, we had our very own hairy potato heads! We had to make sure it was done on the first day of camp so that by the end of the week our potatoes actually had hair! The campers' anticipation each day was adorable.

The timing of the activities during the camp day is important. If you are going to dye eggs for an activity, have the campers put their eggs in the dye as they come in the door. While reading *An Egg Is Quiet* by Dianna Hutts Aston, we had campers drop their hard-boiled egg in whatever color dye they wanted. At the beginning of the day, we also had eggs in soda, water, vinegar, and bleach to show how these interacted with the shells. The dyed eggs were then part of snack time that day. We ensured that when it was time for the egg activity, the eggs had been sitting for a long while.

Every activity has to be fun. An easy way that we build excitement around the activity is through the dialogue with each other as we are doing the read aloud. One example of this was when we were reading the book *Yum! MMMM! Que Rico!: Americas' Sproutings* by Pat Mora, and a question came up about determining the difference between a fruit and a vegetable. We took that opportunity for one of us to go to the computer right then and find an answer to the question. The campers loved hearing what defines a fruit, and then a lively debate ensued about how that classification was not always true. This provided us with an opportunity to model how we get answers to questions that arise. It also shows the campers that it is OK to ask questions as they come up, and we can stop reading to find answers. Finishing the book with no interruptions is not a priority. The student interests and curiosity sometimes drive the direction of the read aloud.

Every activity has to have some kind of "wow" factor. Every activity needs to be something the campers will talk about at home that night and make them want to come back again in the morning. Much of how fun an activity will be depends on the director's attitude. If you can present an activity with enthusiasm, the campers will be excited about doing it. We always banter back and forth about the activity. The enthusiasm of the directors and junior counselors builds excitement for the activity.

Craft activities are easy to present as fun—it's the academic activities that are sometimes a challenge for creating enthusiasm. When doing an academic activity, we try to find a way to make it sizzle. When we did a biography project with the book *Marvelous Maddie: How Margaret E. Knight Became an Inventor* by Emily Arnold McCully, we had web information bookmarked about various inventors. At this time, we were not teaching how to research fully through databases and the Internet, but were focusing on the process itself. We try to make the process something they have not encountered in their regular classrooms, and our expectations for the project are not what they would be during the school year. We want campers to have an experience with the Internet tools without the pressure of a graded project. The finished product will not always be what they would turn in for a grade because we are focusing on the process, rather than the end product. We let campers work in pairs or groups. By using groups, the higher-achieving students can help those who struggle, and there is no pressure to finish something as there would be if the project were for a grade.

Another thing we look at closely is the potential cost of an activity. Some activities don't cost anything, but others can be quite expensive. You need to be careful of the costs of the activities because that can eat up any profits that might be made. If you are doing this as a nonprofit endeavor, your expenses can get high. You should plan in your budget how much or what percentage of your earnings you want to spend on activities. Once we find an activity, we study it thoroughly to make sure it is financially feasible. We may have to alter the original activity to make it affordable. There are many ways to make an idea work. The end product may have to be smaller, a different color, or made out of a different material than originally planned. Keep your activities flexible and creative. Some parts of the activity may have to be purchased in bulk. You may need to do an activity with a different product than you had originally planned. Sometimes we find if we do a little extra work upfront, we can still do the activity. If we find a kit of some sort that we like as an activity, we study the kit and see whether we can do it cheaper by purchasing the pieces in bulk. If we can't, we order kits. We try not to have too many "kit activities." We don't want our camp to be too ready-made.

Types of Activities

In this section, we have divided activities into several categories: crafts, games, experiments, research, and information sharing.

Crafts

We use the term "craft" for anything that involves paper, glue, scissors, paint, markers, construction paper, butcher paper, and the like and for something that usually would not be assigned as a homework project. Some craft projects are inspired by a trip to the local craft store. You just need to open your imagination to what you can do with grassy moss and glue or cut scrapbook paper. Our craft projects often start with a dream of what the outcome will be, and then we work backward to figure out how to do it! Here are some craft activities we've done in the past.

Dogs Made Out of Dog Biscuits

These darling little creatures were LARGE dog biscuits for the body with googley eyes, felt ears, a red pom-pom nose, a beaded mouth, and a cute little ribbon around the neck. Campers also made their "pets" little beds, which could be either a jewelry pouch or a library cardholder.

Pillow Cases

To go along with a book about bedrooms and pajamas, we made pillowcases the size of travel pillows. We got the cheapest white fabric we could find, stitched up cases, and printed each one with "Camp Bluebonnet '00" and a camper's name with a paint pen. Then we had the campers decorate the cases with acrylic paint using sponges for stamping and brushes for painting. When doing this activity, we monitored the amount of paint campers used so the pillowcases would dry quickly. We then took them home and put them in the dryer so the paint could set, and the campers took them home at the end of the week. We have gotten reports for a couple of years that the pillows were still on campers' beds or went on vacation with them!

Pop-Up Cards

To accompany a pop-up book, we watched a video about how pop-up books are produced. We found it on the Internet at a site that we could access from school. The website also featured instructions for making adorable pop-up cards. We made a simple one with a heart that leapt out, as well as a more complicated two-piece birthday cake. Working very slowly and with lots of reminders to "do exactly as I tell you," these cards worked out terrifically. We had the campers color them with regular crayons instead of markers so that they would be a little more subtle than regular marker-colored cards.

Potato Prints

For this project, we gave each camper half a potato, a plastic knife, paper, and paint. They carved a design out of their potato to create a stamp, and then, dipping the potatoes in paint, they stamped away on the paper. They could share their stamps with their friends and create different designs on their paper. They could wipe off their potato and do different colors. Large 11 x 17 paper or computer paper is good for this project.

Paper-Bag Scrapbooks

Using paper lunch sacks, the campers created a paper scrapbook in which they glued pictures they had brought from home. We had lots of scrapbook paper and various other items available to decorate their books. The sacks provided a pocket where campers could put little treasures or write details about the pictures they used for their books. Some campers wrote a story in their book rather than use it as a scrapbook.

Space Necklace

This is one example of when we used a purchased kit for an activity. The kit came with colored wooden beads and shapes related to space, such as planets, rockets, and stars. The campers used glitter paint to decorate the beads and shapes, then strung them onto a black cord.

Colorful Paper-Towel Roll Maracas

This is an oldie but goodie. We gathered empty paper-towel rolls ahead of time and precut paper to fit around the rolls. Each camper decorated the paper with markers, then Junior Counselors (whom we discuss in greater detail in the next chapter) helped them tape the paper to the roll, including a square for each end. Before the second square was taped on, the roll was filled with rice, beans, or a combination of both depending on the camper's preference. We then used the maracas as we danced in a conga line around the library!

Games

Many books lend themselves to good old-fashioned games. We have discovered that kids just want to be kids and play. That is not a revolutionary insight, but one we go back to regularly. Our campers like to race each other, help each other find things, and repeat tried-and-true rhymes. Games are fun to do all week long when the campers have extra time. We never put away the jump ropes or mummy wraps. The campers can't get enough of them! Following are some game activities we've done in the past.

Jump-Rope Rhymes

The campers love this because they don't have the same opportunity to jump rope anymore. So much of their outside recess time is prescripted play. We provided each camper with a jump rope to use during camp and take home at the end. We used long jump ropes so the campers could do group jumping. The Junior Counselors were excellent jump rope turners and taught the campers how to turn the ropes. We found some good jump rope rhyme books in our collection that included some new rhymes as well as the good old traditional rhymes. Both boys and girls loved this and did it during every spare moment throughout the week.

Potato Races

It seems like we've had lots of potato books on our camp reading lists. Campers love to race each other, and there are lots of appropriate activities for the potato theme. We used potatoes in several types of races. One was the traditional potato-on-a-spoon relay race. We used large spoons and little potatoes for this. In another race, two campers put a potato between their backs and had to cross the finish line without dropping their potato. The campers also played a potato toss where after each toss, they move back a step. They tossed until one team was left that had not dropped their potato. Lastly the campers put a potato under their chin and passed it from camper to camper in a circle.

Mummy Wrapping

We originally planned on making this a race to see who could wrap their mummy the fastest. However, the campers had so much fun just wrapping each other that we let them have at it. We calculated how many rolls of toilet paper it would take to do this and decided it would be too expensive and not environmentally sound. So we used scrap material cut in 4-inch-wide strips that were very long. Each strip was sewn together to create 15-foot-long strips for each team to use to wrap their partner from head to toe. Each camper had a turn being both the wrapper and the mummy.

Flashlight Tag

Each camper was asked to bring a flashlight on a specific day. When it was time to play tag, they got out their flashlights, and we dimmed the lights as much as possible. Each camper used his or her flashlight to "tag" other campers. If you were tagged, you had to sit down until someone freed you by touching you. The campers really enjoyed the fact that they got to run in the library. We made sure to bring extra flashlights for those who didn't have one. The campers even came up with their own variations on the game.

Experiments

Once in a while, we run across a book that lends itself to a science experiment, although when we say "science experiment," we use that term very loosely. There isn't a lot of time at a reading camp to do an in-depth ten-step experiment, so be careful what you attempt. We rarely talk about the scientific method, so if you are a true science kind of person, be careful how far you go into a project. We keep these activities fun and simple. If there is an experiment that will take several days to accomplish or to see the results, make sure it is started early in the week. The more time you have to see the fruits of your work, the more fun the campers have with the activity. Here are some experiment activities we've done in the past.

Dinosaur Artifacts

To go along with a dinosaur book, we put little plastic dinosaurs in a Dixie cup and filled it with plaster of Paris. We tore the paper cup off, leaving what seemed like just a lump of plaster. We gave each one of the campers one of these lumps, as well as a hammer, and let them loose. We talked to them about how an archeologist wouldn't just go blasting away at a site when they didn't know what was inside it. So they started out hammering away very gingerly. After a while, it did take some force, but it was certainly fun. Fortunately, one of our fathers had a collection of antique hammers we could use.

Also, to go along with the dinosaur unit, we hid larger plastic dinosaur eggs in the sand volleyball pit. The campers had to dig them out, like a hidden egg hunt. This was fun for the morning group, but in Texas, it is really hot outside on summer afternoons, but we endured the heat and dug away. We also made sure we knew where in the volleyball pit the "artifacts" were buried so we could find them all.

Painting Like an Elephant

To go along with a book about elephants dancing a ballet in a circus, we learned about an organization that raises money to help save elephants in Africa. The group actually has elephants paint on canvas and then sells the paintings for a lot of money. We paired the campers so that one was the trainer and one was the elephant. With a piece of paper taped on the wall, the "elephant" held the paintbrush in his or her mouth, and the "trainer" gave signals as to what design to paint. Of course, everyone got to play both parts. After their paintings were dry, we mounted them in mat-board frames to take home. The "elephants" had to tell us which side was up!

Potato Heads or Shrunken Heads

Campers each got a potato with the top hollowed out. They decorated their potatoes with various odds and ends to create a face. Then they put a mixture of potting soil and rye grass seeds into the hollowed-out area. These were placed on paper plates and put in the sunlight. Each camper was responsible for watering his or her potato head each morning. By the end of the week, there were some hairy potato heads. Campers enjoyed watching the progression as the hair grew and the potato heads shrunk.

Research

Doing research can be a lot of fun when it is presented as an enjoyable activity. Anything "school-like" should be fun, fun, fun! We always step back and look at a research activity and ask ourselves whether it looks too much like school. If it does, the campers will balk at it. We have used resources from our print section of the library as well as online database or well-defined and monitored searches. One year, we actually had our school's computer-on-wheels lab with enough computers for each camper to have his or her own laptop. That doesn't always happen, so we use all the available computers in the library. The campers love to team up on a project. It is a good idea if you can team up stronger students with the not-quite-as-strong students. There is not always a lot of time for in-depth research, so you need to guide the students to just the right place. As noted earlier in the chapter, we guide students with premade wikis or bookmarks on the computers. Some research activities may be completely pre-made and the campers just have to cut and paste and make pretty.

We have the campers share what they have done so that everyone benefits from each other's discoveries. This always starts a lively discussion. It is fun to watch the campers interacting about the things they have learned in their research, and they don't even realize it is an academic project! Sometimes you need to look at the activity and decide which is more important, the process or the end product. Once again, we cannot stress enough, remember to keep it fun. Its summer, so don't worry about the "A" paper! Here are some research activities we've done in the past.

WWII Timeline

To illustrate the timeline of what happened during World War II, we had the campers work in teams to make a long timeline on butcher paper. We facilitated an information-sharing session about the events of WWII. The students were then given resources including websites to use in choosing which events they wanted to include on their timelines. They printed pictures and glued them onto the butcher paper in chronological order. The groups added a title and were free to decorate their timelines however they wanted. Some of the campers did vertical timelines, and others did horizontal timelines. We hung the end products around the library to share and compare.

Biography

We did biography reports about African American inventors. We purchased large biography poster report forms, but you can make your own. Campers researched their inventors and filled in their posters. The posters included boxes for things such as a portrait, quotes, life lessons, facts, and resources, as well as a film reel to draw inventors' life stories.

Observation Information Page

After reading a book about Native Americans, we directed the campers to websites about the Trail of Tears. They saw pictures of the event and filled out an observation page with questions such as, What did you see? and Who was in the picture? We also told them to describe the expressions on the faces of the Native Americans on the Trail. Campers then read some personal accounts of people who were on the Trail of Tears and answered questions about those narratives.

Information Sharing

Sometimes a topic lends itself to informing campers about a subject with which they may not be familiar, or we just want to stir up a topic for discussion. One of us is great at putting together informative PowerPoint presentations. This is where we really team up well. We both can find the information and both can talk a topic to death, and fortunately one of us is good at putting together a forum to facilitate that conversation. Many times, this becomes one of the best parts of camp. Everyone is learning about a new subject, sharing opinions, discussing the facts, and forming new opinions. It is all of us learning together. It is always a good day when a camper teaches us something or we see that spark in a camper's eye that says "I want to know more!"

One way to share information is for the campers to create their own PowerPoint presentations on a topic. This gives them the opportunity to learn a new computer skill or hone one they have learned. Working with a program that is used regularly in classrooms is a good way to enhance the campers' knowledge base. They are learning and don't even know it! It is always fun to have the campers share what they have created. Here are some information-sharing activities we've done in the past.

Pale Male

A PowerPoint presentation with actual footage was created to show the life of the red-tailed hawk, Pale Male, in New York City. It included information on Central Park and red-tailed hawks in general, as well as specific information on the history of Pale Male. We used this as a springboard to compare and contrast life in New York with that in Texas.

Paper versus Plastic

A PowerPoint presentation was used to learn information about reusing and recycling. After thoroughly discussing the pros and cons of plastic and paper bags, we took a vote on which was better to use. Then we gave them another option: reusable bags. Afterward, each camper decorated his or her own reusable bag to take home and use to protect the environment. This discussion provided the opportunity to use fact versus opinion and how to use facts to support opinions.

Reader's Theater

Reader's theater is a dramatic enactment of text. It is an oral activity in which campers read a script and practice reading their part with fluency and intonation. Unlike traditional theater, the emphasis is mainly on the oral expression of the part. We almost always include one reader's theater activity in camp week.

We are lucky that the Texas Library Association creates reader's theater scripts each year for several of the books on the Bluebonnet list. Some years we have created our own by taking the book and turning it into narration and dialogue. It is easy to create your own script for any of the books you choose to use at your camp. It can also work well to have your campers create their own scripts from a given book. It is fun because each group develops something different.

We divide the campers into groups of four or five. We give them the script and time to practice. We also provide basic supplies to use to create any props they want, such as butcher paper, scissors, tape, markers, and so on. Props are not required, but some groups have gotten really creative with this. When we did the reader's theater for the book *Pale Male: Citizen Hawk of New York City* by Janet Schulman, one group created picket signs to use, another group created the New York skyline, and another had a boy on crutches that turned into hawk wings!

After the groups have had about thirty minutes to practice, we all move to the story area, where the groups take turns presenting their reader's theater. It is always fun to see how each group interprets the parts. We don't expect it to be perfect, and the campers can use the printed script if needed. Again, the focus is on the process and having fun—not the end product.

Choosing Your Activities

When choosing the activities for your camp, keep several things in mind.

Questions to think about:

- How long will this activity take?

- Is it age appropriate?

- What materials will you need to complete the activity?

- Are the activities varied enough each day?

- Is there enough balance between fun and academic projects?

- Is each activity fun?

- Can you get any of the items donated?

- Do you want to have the students choose an activity and plan it themselves?

You have your activities all planned. Now you'll need some help to see that those activities run smoothly. The next step is to recruit Junior Counselor volunteers to help run your camp, and that's the topic of our next chapter.

Chapter 4

Selecting Junior Counselor Volunteers

SUMMER CAMP

One of the things we learned quickly—and if we recall, quite painfully—when we first began planning a reading camp is that we needed more than just the two of us to actually run the camp. This chapter is intended to help you choose the right volunteers for that job. We call our volunteers "Junior Counselors."

Helpers, Assistants, and Volunteers

We were successful in planning our camp, but we realized we were going to need some extra hands to execute it. Since one of our goals was to supplement our income, we set out to recruit some young students who were in need of some community service hours rather than pay assistants to help us. You can always use middle and high school students who are looking for community service hours; you just have to find those students. We have had several helpers at several different ages, and there is no tried or true age or gender determination of what works best. As you probably know, you never know someone until he or she works for you. All the Junior Counselors are sent a letter before the camp starts outlining their responsibilities and what is expected of them. This way, there is never a question about what they are expected to do (see Appendix F). We recruit through friends' children, former campers, former students, fellow teachers' children, and the National Honor Society at middle or high schools. We are always on the lookout for individuals who might want to have a great volunteer experience, whether it is for their resumé or just a break from getting bored with summer. We rely on the fact that students need volunteer hours for so many things these days, and the reality is that young people can only watch so much TV or hang out with their friends for so long before they realize they need to be doing something. We always write fabulous recommendation letters for all the helpers. Some letters just happen to be longer and more glowing than others. We also have former campers who come back and want to help. We actually overheard a couple of the fifth graders at camp whispering about whether they thought they could come back as Junior Counselors the next year!

Boy Versus Girl Volunteers

We wish there was a steadfast rule here. Believe us, we do not mean to generalize or stereotype genders, but, the reality is, boys and girls are different, as campers or as helpers.

With girls, you need to look for maturity and willingness to help before you go any further. With boys you need to look for maturity and willingness to get their hands dirty. Generally we ask for a one-week commitment from the volunteers. This way, if either the camp directors or the Junior Counselors do not like the way things are going, we can cut the cord more easily.

Girl helpers are usually more organized and tend to anticipate what needs to be done next, whether it is setting up snacks or getting supplies out for the next activity. The girls also tend to enjoy doing the activities, so their enthusiasm spills over into the campers' excitement. We try to have enough supplies so the volunteers can create their own projects.

A girl with an attitude, regardless of age, is going to be hard to deal with. If in the middle of the week you realize you are dealing with someone who is not willing to help because she is "too cool," you must find something for her to do away from the group. Otherwise, her bad attitude will filter into your campers and the other Junior Counselors. We have had some girls volunteer for us whom we thought we knew, but once students have left elementary school for middle school, their attitudes can change.

With boys, we have discovered, maturity is not necessarily a factor. The boys we have had volunteer for our camp can really get on board with challenging boy campers to do the activities. If the boy campers see an older boy jumping rope or doing the samba, they are more willing to jump right in! We have had some middle-school-boy Junior Counselors who have bribed campers with snacks or playtime to get them to write an extra poem or letter. At first we were not really sure this was a good idea, but it did keep the campers motivated when they were faced with something that looked academic! Boys are also adept at turning an activity into a competition, whether it was intended to be one or not. Who can jump rope the fastest, longest, funniest? Who can make the funniest folder art? Who can make the face on his potato head the cleverest? We are constantly amazed at how boys can make a game out of anything.

Younger versus Older

Again, we wish there was a steadfast rule for what age is a good age for helping! Some helpers are just naturally good at assisting. They are the ones who anticipate your next move or what needs to be done for tomorrow's lesson, or who see that in five minutes we are going to be having snacks, and it is time to move in that direction. Other helpers need to be taught this skill. We tell our Junior Counselors in the beginning that we are going to tell them what needs to be done and they are going to be responsible for carrying out the tasks they are given. With that said, we have had twelve year olds who could handle the task and seventeen year olds who could not. We are very careful to make sure the younger Junior Counselors are aware of what they are getting into before they say "yes" to volunteering. If they have been campers before, they know what to expect, and this is a good thing. Regardless of age, this is a good opportunity for children to learn the art of volunteerism. We think it is our responsibility to guide them.

How Many?

The number of helpers you have depends partially on the size of your camp and partially on how helpful your helpers are. We like to have four or five Junior Counselors for each camp session of twenty students. This is a good number because there are enough Junior Counselors to be assisting with an activity while the others are getting ready for snack time or the next activity. It is also enough so that when there is some lag time, they can visit.

At the end of the camp week, we try to recognize the Junior Counselors for their volunteer service. We also give them something to say "thank you," usually a gift card and maybe pizza delivered for lunch.

It is important to recruit good volunteers so that everything runs smoothly. After you've jumped this hurdle, it's time for one more task to prepare for the big event: choosing the snacks you will offer campers during their week with you. Suggestions for snacks and how they can align with your activities are provided in the next chapter.

Chapter 5

Snacks

SNACKS ARE THEME RELATED AND NOT NECESSARILY NUTRITIOUS

During your reading camp, you must offer a snack every day, and every day the snack must be fun, exciting, and delicious! It is also imperative that you make three things clear to parents before camp starts.

First, on our original marketing flyer, we are very clear that *the snacks at camp are not necessarily nutritious but are theme related.* Many states and school districts mandate that during the school day, you may not have foods that are of minimal nutritious value. During camp, we inform everyone up front that there is nothing nutritious about our day. It is just about impossible to make a Lock Ness monster out of anything other than a gummy worm. And how else would you talk about how potato chips were invented if you didn't fry your own chips?

This is probably the funnest part of planning camp. Coming up with snacks to go with each theme is usually "a piece of cake." Everyone likes to eat, and we all like to play with our food sometimes. The campers begin guessing what the snack will be when they hear which book we are reading for the day. The more creative you are, the more they will enjoy it.

Second, be sure to let parents know if you will be using any cooking utensils or devices that might be considered unsafe. For example, each year we have a fried snack. The campers love it because hardly anyone fries at home these days, and most of the children have never seen a deep fryer. One of us found a new deep fryer on sale after the holidays one year, so we purchased it and use it all the time. We assure parents that the frying is done in the office by only one of us. If the campers come in to look or to drop their own pastry design into the oil, we do all the work and keep them at a *very* safe distance. This goes for the junior counselors as well. Keep safety concerns in mind when using any kitchen device that might be dangerous around children.

A third and very important issue is food allergies. Generally, if you have a student who is allergic to a food, the parents and child are very eager to tell you about it. We also ask directly about food allergies and other medical issues on our registration form (see Appendix A). We always have an alternative snack available for children with allergies, or sometimes the parent offers to send one snack. For some reason, we always wind up using peanut butter for at least one day. You need to make sure you know whether you are in a peanut-free school before camp planning starts.

When planning your snacks, you need to consider several factors, including time, cost, messiness, prep time, cleanup time, and how you are going to serve them.

Two supplies that are critical for snack time are box or pouch juices and coffee filters. We purchase all the box/pouch juices ahead of time for the week. You will be amazed at the number of juice boxes you go through. When you first go to purchase them and you realize one box per student per session is one hundred juice boxes and you are buying for three camp sessions, it does seem a bit overwhelming, but just get out the flatbed roller and stack them up. The campers don't ever seem to be picky about what the brand is or whether they are boxes or pouches. We just go for what is the most economical for purchasing three hundred juices at the same time! We get a variety of choices in the same brand and have them ready to go at the beginning of each day. Keeping the juice supply ready is an excellent duty for the junior counselors. Have an ice chest in the snack area, purchase ice every couple of days, and have the junior counselors fill the ice chest with juices as their last task in the afternoon. That way, the juices are ready for the next morning.

We have also discovered the campers are not really picky about the juices being cold, and they have never complained about the variety available to them. We usually have two different kinds of juices in the ice chest, and campers choose one or the other. During snack time, the campers can take one juice, after that they are offered water.

Coffee filters are the best, cheapest way to deliver snacks. They are shaped like a bowl, are absorbent, don't cost much money, and don't hurt the environment when we throw them away. Whether we are having popcorn or chips, snacks are easily placed in the coffee filters to be delivered to the campers. If we are doing a snack that needs to be assembled, we put all the various parts and pieces in the coffee filter for the campers. Many times, the recipe for the day's snack is included in the campers' daily work packet. This helps when they want to share the recipe with their parents. Following are some of examples of the best snacks ever.

- Homemade potato chips (*George Crum*)

- Fresh popcorn in paper bags (*Marvelous Mattie*)

- Oatmeal cookies with icing and Loch Ness Monster gummy worms (*The Luck of the Loch Ness Monster*)

- "Puppy chow": sometimes you can find this recipe on Chex cereal boxes. It is a combination of peanut butter, chocolate, and powdered sugar on Chex cereal. This is a must-do snack. (*Help Me, Mr. Mutt* and other dog-themed books)

- Indian fry bread (*Crossing Bok Chitto*)

- Fruit kabobs (*Yum! Mmmm! Que Rico!*)

Considerations when picking snacks include the following:

- How will you get the snacks from the prep area to the students?

  - Cart

  - Trays

  - Junior counselors hand carry them

  - Students come to the prep area

- Do you want the snack to be healthy?

- Where are you getting your ideas for snacks?

  - Internet search

  - Children's cookbooks

  - Recipes in the featured book

(Note: A new book by Melissa Rosetti, *Story Times Good Enough to Eat!: Thematic Programs with Edible Story Crafts* [Libraries Unlimited, 2010], may give you an idea for a food craft even if you don't use the books she has chosen for the snack.)

You have selected the books you'll read, you've found your junior volunteers, your registration is complete, and your setting is prepared. Now it's opening day!

Chapter 6

Opening Day

All your planning is complete. Now it's time for camp! This chapter describes what you'll need for opening day.

Supplies

You will need a few basic supplies on hand for camp. Some are for activities, some are for setup, and some are for making sure things run smoothly. If there are any leftovers, we store them, and we now have several boxes of supplies that we can pull out for future camps. Once a group of campers has cycled through and a new book about an old subject comes back on our list, we can always pull out an old activity.

Basic supplies for camp are scissors, markers, glue sticks, and pencils. We try to stock up on these things during the back-to-school sales and store them for camp. It never hurts to have a few extra markers, and it surely is miserable if you run out of glue sticks! We keep a small plastic tub on each table with the basic supplies. No one wants to be running around gathering markers or scissors for every activity. Also, if the basics are readily available all the time, anytime there is a lull, the campers can go back to their daily packets or to previous activities they have in their folders.

Supplies for projects and activities are purchased ahead of schedule and kept in our holding area. Supplies for specific activities should be purchased in large quantities to get a better price. We purchase enough supplies for all the campers who are signed up and then a few extras. We never want to run short of a supply because we had a last-minute camper show up or because a camper botched an activity so badly it couldn't be rescued.

Supplies for setup can be things such as colored paper for registration fliers, nice card stock for certificates, ink for printers, and name tags. We bit the bullet and bought clip-on name tags a couple of years ago, so the campers can have them every day. Because we run our camp at two schools, we don't know every camper in each session. We also have campers from schools other than our own who have come with a friend or have heard about us through the grapevine. We always want those campers to feel welcome and part of the group.

To keep camp running smoothly, we suggest every camper have a manila folder. As suggested earlier, we use legal size because most of our activities can fit in them for safekeeping during the week.

Preparing for Opening Day

The goal for the first day is for everything to go as smoothly as possible. The day before your camp starts, go to your campsite and get everything laid out. Make sure all your areas are clearly defined and ready to go. In each area, make sure you have all the supplies you'll need. We have a story area, an opening/activity/snack area, a computer area, and a snack prep area.

The opening area is where you will greet the campers each morning. We have a sign-in sheet and name tags already filled out. As noted earlier, we invested in clip-on plastic ones so we can reuse them each day. On the first day, campers can decorate them if they want. You can show the campers where to check in each day. At the opening area, they can also pick up their folders and packets. Each camper has a legal-size manila folder with his or her name on it, which they can also decorate if they wish. The daily activity packet should be inside the folder, ready to go.

The activity area is usually a group of tables where campers can sit and do all their activities. After they have checked in, they can go sit at these tables and get busy visiting with friends and working on their daily activity packet. On the activity tables, we always have a basket of markers. These stay out all week because they are used constantly. In the activity area, we also have a counter where the items we need for the day are stored. Whatever is needed for the day's activities is put there, including tape, scissors, construction paper, glue, or whatever other items are necessary.

The computer area is wherever you have your bank of computers. As we have discussed in previous chapters, we have a wiki for each day's theme. On the wiki, we include several activities for the day's theme, and we can add to it easily as we come across more Internet activities. The URL of the wiki is on the front of the campers' daily packet, so when they go home, they can look at it there.

The snack prep area is usually away from any of the camp activities. The library office works well for this because there is a sink and it is away from the children. If we are going to do any cooking, we set that up in the office as well. It is helpful to have some kind of rolling cart to move the food from the preparation area to the eating area.

We also set up a white board in the story area with the day's agenda on it so that the campers can anticipate the timing of the activities. It also keeps us somewhat on track!

An example of one of our weeks is provided in the next chapter.

Chapter 7

Example of a Day at Camp

Now let's take it step by step through a typical half-day camp session. This will give you a feel for the flow of the day so you can anticipate and plan for each step.

- Meet and greet (15 minutes)

    - As campers arrive, they receive a folder full of activities and their name badges. They find a spot, decorate their folders, and begin working on activity pages found in the folder. We use this time to communicate with parents and get to know the campers.

- Story Time (20–30 minutes)

    - The campers gather in the story area, where we have the agenda for the day, the day's storybook, and a collection of titles that correlate with the topic.

    - We begin by booktalking several of the other books on the list. We read a passage from each book we don't use to get campers interested in reading the other books on the list.

    - Read the book of the day.

    - Junior counselors are preparing for our first activity at this time.

- Activity I (30–45 minutes)

    - Campers move to the area for their first activity.

    - When the activity is completed, the campers and Junior Counselors help clean up the area.

- Snack (15 minutes)

    - Junior counselors pass out the snacks. Campers go to the ice chest to get their drinks. Campers can work on their folders during this time.

    - Campers are expected to clean up after themselves.

- Activity II (30–45 minutes)

    - Campers move to the area for their second activity.

- Clean up (15 minutes)

    - Campers clean up all activities.

    - Campers can complete any unfinished projects.

    - Campers put everything in their folders and get things ready to take home.

    - Folders stay at camp, as do some of the activities that don't go home until the end of the week.

- Closing (15 minutes)

    - Campers gather at the story area where we read part of the chapter book of the week.

    - Junior counselors clean up for the day and prepare for the next day.

The first day will be just a little different as name badges are found and decorated, and the campers learn how to check in on the roster. The campers make friends and find where they like to sit.

On the last day of camp, be sure to leave enough time to wrap up the chapter book and pass out "Certificates of Participation" (Appendix G). Certificates are made earlier in the week on any print-shop software. On the last day, all projects and the now well-stocked daily folder all go home!

Conclusion

The reading camp program we have presented in this short book can be used in so many different formats.

If you are a public librarian, these ideas are perfect to help plan a summer program full of storytimes and activities.

If you are a homeschooler these ideas will help you plan your curriculum—both during the year and in the summer.

If you are a classroom teacher, these ideas are great for enriching a language arts curriculum.

If you are a parent, these ideas give you an opportunity to spend some quality time reading with your child. This is the perfect way to show your child fun activities and keep reading over the summer.

If you are a public school librarian, you can use these ideas to create a literature night at your school.

You just need to pick your setting, pick your books, and jump in with both feet. You really can't make a mistake because it's your camp and your ideas.

We have given you all the tools you'll need to be successful. Just be sure to take the time to plan ahead. Grab a friend, get started, and have fun!

Appendix A

Registration Form and Payment Reminder Form

Camp Summer Read

Located at the Gullett Library   6310 Treadwell Blvd.

Spend a fun filled week with next year's Bluebonnet books through reading, exploring, creating & discussing the 2009-2010 Bluebonnet books. By the end of the week campers will be qualified to vote for next year's Bluebonnet Award and be well on their way!!

$125 per session fee includes all materials and a daily snack*

The camp will be taught by Gullett librarian, Kay Gooch and HaysCISD librarian, Charlotte Massey.

Each camp is limited to 20 participants to ensure a low camper to teacher ratio.

*Snacks are theme related - not necessarily nutritious!

To reserve your child's space, return the bottom portion of this note along with a $25 nonrefundable deposit to your child's teacher.

Please make checks out to **Kay Gooch.**

The remainder of the fee will be due on the last week of school, May 25, 2010.

Please indicate your first and second choice:

___July 12 - 16: 1:00 - 4:00 pm   **or** ___ July 19 - 23: 9:00 am – 12:00 noon   **or** ___ July 19 - 23: 1:00 - 4:00 pm

child's name _____current teacher _____

parent name _____phone #s_____

address_____e-mail_____

emergency contact_____phone #s_____

doctor_____phone # _____

Who will pick your child up from camp?_____

Does your child have any food allergies, medical problems, or other issues we should be aware of?

_____

Camp Bluebonnet

_____ is registered
for the morning session July 12–19, 9:00 a.m.–noon.

Our records show that you have paid $_____.

$_____ is due by Thursday, May 25. Please make all checks to Kay
Gooch.

See you July 12, 9:00 a.m. at the Gullett Library!!

Camp Bluebonnet

_____ is registered
for the morning session July 12–19, 9:00 a.m.–noon.

Our records show that you have paid $_____.

$_____ is due by Thursday, May 25. Please make all checks to Kay
Gooch.

See you July 12, 9:00 a.m. at the Gullett Library!!

Appendix B

Books Used at Camp Summer Read

Borden, Louise. *The Greatest Skating Race: A World War II Story from the Netherlands*. Margaret K. McElderry, 2004. ISBN-13: 978-0-689-84502-4

    Notes: During World War II in the Netherlands, a ten-year-old boy's dream of skating in a famous race allows him to help two children escape to Belgium by ice-skating past German soldiers and other enemies.

Deedy, Carmen Agra. *Martina the Beautiful Cockroach: A Cuban Folktale*. Peachtree, 2007. ISBN-13: 978-1-56145-399-3

    Notes: A humorous retelling of a Cuban folktale in which a cockroach interviews her suitors to decide whom to marry.

DeFelice, Cynthia C. *One Potato, Two Potato*. Farrar, Straus & Giroux, 2006. ISBN-13: 978-0-374-35640-8

    Notes: A very poor, humble couple lives so simple a life that they share everything, until the husband discovers a pot with magical powers buried under the very last potato in the garden.

Flaherty, Alice. *The Luck of the Loch Ness Monster: A Tale of Picky Eating*. Houghton Mifflin, 2007. ISBN-13: 978-0-618-55644-1

    Notes: A young American girl's picky eating habits transform a small worm into the famous Loch Ness monster.

Florian, Douglas. *Comets, Stars, the Moon, and Mars: Space Poems and Paintings*. Harcourt, 2007. ISBN-13: 978-0-15-205372-7

> **Notes:** A collection of twenty whimsical poems about comets, the stars, the moon, and the planets. Includes bibliographical references.

Lauber, Patricia. *What You Never Knew About Beds, Bedrooms, and Pajamas*. Simon & Schuster Books for Young Readers, 2006. ISBN-13: 978-0-689-85211-4

> **Notes:** Includes bibliographical references. Presents facts on where people have slept and what they have slept on and in throughout history, covering such settings as the Stone Age; ancient Egypt, Greece, and Rome; and medieval Europe.

Markle, Sandra. *Outside and Inside Mummies*. Walker, 2005. ISBN-13: 978-0-8027-8967-9

> **Notes:** Describes the technology used to uncover the many secrets of mummies, including how they died and their age, as well as the diet of the ancient Egyptians.

McCully, Emily Arnold. *Marvelous Mattie: How Margaret E. Knight Became an Inventor*. Farrar, Straus & Giroux, 2006. ISBN-13: 978-0-374-34810-6

> **Notes:** Includes bibliographical references. Describes inventor Margaret E. Knight's childhood, explaining how her interest in mechanical innovations began, and tells the story of her invention of a paper-bag maker and her legal battle for the patent after someone stole her idea.

Mora, Pat. *Yum! Mmmm! Que Rico!: Americas' Sproutings*. Lee & Low Books Inc., 2007. ISBN-13: 978-1-58430-271-1

> **Notes:** Includes bibliographical references. A collection of haikus that celebrates indigenous foods of the Americas, such as blueberries and vanilla, and includes information about each food's origins.

Osborne, Mary Pope. *Pompeii: Lost & Found*. Knopf, 2006. ISBN-13: 978-0-375-82889-8

> **Notes:** Presents a short, illustrated narrative of the city of Pompeii before the A.D. 79 eruption of Mount Vesuvius buried the city and describes how, in 1763, the city was rediscovered.

Schubert, Leda. *Ballet of the Elephants*. Roaring Brook Press, 2006. ISBN-13: 978-1-59643-075-4

> **Notes:** "A Deborah Brodie book." Includes bibliographical references. Tells the story of how circus owner John Ringling North, choreographer George Balanchine, and composer Igor Stravinsky teamed up to create the *Circus Polka,* a ballet for fifty elephants and fifty dancers, and describes the opening night performance in 1942.

Schulman, Janet. *Pale Male: Citizen Hawk of New York City*. Knopf, 2008. ISBN-13: 978-0-375-94558-8

> **Notes:** Includes bibliographical references. Recounts the true story of Pale Male, a red-tailed hawk living in New York City who has become one of the city's most-watched celebrities. Bird watchers, tourists, and residents admire the bird and his nest, built on a Fifth Avenue apartment building.

Stevens, Janet. *Help Me, Mr. Mutt!: Expert Answers for Dogs with People Problems*. Harcourt, 2008. ISBN-13: 978-0-15-204628-6

> **Notes:** Dogs across the United States write to Mr. Mutt, a people expert, for help with their humans.

Taylor, Gaylia. *George Crum and the Saratoga Chip.* Lee & Low Books, 2006. ISBN-13: 978-1-58430-255-1

> **Notes:** Describes chef George Crum's childhood as a part Native American, part African American boy in rural 1830s New York, his adventures cooking at Moon's Lake House restaurant in Sarasota Springs, and his accidental invention of one of America's most beloved snacks. Includes bibliographical references.

Tingle, Tim. *Crossing Bok Chitto: A Choctaw Tale of Friendship & Freedom.* Cinco Puntos Press, 2006. ISBN-13: 978-0-938317-77-7

> **Notes:** In the 1800s, a Choctaw girl becomes friends with a slave boy from a plantation across the great river, and when she learns that his family is in trouble, she helps them cross to freedom.

Appendix C

Book Planning Forms

Book Planning Form

Title: *Pale Male: Citizen Hawk of New York*
ISBN: 978-0-375-94558-8
Author: Jane Schulman
E-mail: kids@random.com
Illustrator: Meilo So
Interview: PaperTigers.org

Synopsis: Recounts the true story of Pale Male, a red-tailed hawk living in New York City who has become one of the city's most-watched celebrities. Bird watchers, tourists, and residents admire the bird and his nest, built on a Fifth Avenue apartment building.

Interesting facts to talk about: Central Park, hawks, apartment buildings in New York City

Activity 1

A: <u>PowerPoint presentation.</u> Presentation includes information about New York City, Central Park (maps, pictures, and facts), red-tailed hawks (pictures and facts), 927 Fifth Avenue apartment building (pictures of building and up-close picture of nest), Pale Male and Lola (pictures of birds), actual footage from Pale Male documentary, and bird nests (close-up pictures of bird nests and what they are made of).

B: <u>Nests for Pale Male.</u> Campers go outside and collect moss, leaves, sticks, twine, and anything that looks like it could be used in a nest. Campers return to the library and receive a handful of moss purchased at a craft store. Campers form nests using all the materials they collected. The nests are taken outside to an adult supervisor, who sprays the nests with spray glue purchased at a craft store. Campers then add a small bird made from a mushroom, also purchased at the craft store. Set aside to dry.

Snack: Candy Bird Nests

Haystacks made from butterscotch or chocolate and chow mien noodles.

Melt 1 cup chocolate chips or butterscotch chips in a double boiler. When melted, combine melted chocolate (or butterscotch) with 1½ cups chow mien noodles in a large mixing bowl. Stir with a wooden spoon. Spoon about ¼ cup of the mixture into a paper cupcake holder and make a small indention in the top. When serving, add a couple of bird eggs to the nest. "Eggs" can be Spring Whoppers, Peanut M&M's, or yogurt-covered almonds.

Activity 2

Reader's Theatre: Divide the campers into groups of four or five. Each group works on its play or skit for about 15 minutes. Campers make props and costumes from butcher paper, construction paper, markers, etc. Each group presents its play to the audience of other campers.

Wiki Information

Audubon Society, Central Park, map of NYC, bird sounds and songs, website with links to many bird sites

Packet Information

Information and coloring page about Red-Tail hawks, Bird Word Find, Birds—A bird name for each letter, writing page, story and picture

Book Planning Form

Title: *One Potato, Two Potato*
ISBN-13: 978-0-374-35640-8
Author: Cynthia C. DeFelice
E-mail: www.cythiadefelice.com
Illustrator: Andrea U'Ren

> **Synopsis:** A very poor, humble couple live so simply that they share everything, until the husband discovers a pot with magical powers buried under the very last potato in their garden.

> **Interesting facts to talk about:** Folktales, exponential notation, old-fashioned hand clapping rhymes

Activity 1

Grass-Growing Potato Head: Each camper gets a small potato with the bottom sliced off so that it stands upright on its own, and the top of the potato has a small "well" carved out to put dirt in it. The campers have access to googly eyes, ribbons, markers, fabric pieces, snack carrots, beads, chenille sticks, and construction paper. Glue, glue guns, and toothpicks are used to attach all decorations for campers to make their own potato faces. (Junior counselors are in charge of the glue gun!) Each camper mixes together potting soil and a teaspoon of rye grass seeds and puts it in the well of the head. Water each day, and by the end of the week, the Potato Heads have hair!

Snack

Store-bought potato chips in a variety of flavors.

Activity 2

Potato Games: These games can be enjoyed inside or outside. A small bag of potatoes and serving-size spoons from your kitchen (plastic spoons are not big or strong enough) are necessary. Set up an area where the campers can run back and forth from start to finish, about 25 yards apart. Line them up in teams in three or four lanes.

1. Back-to-Back: Campers stand back-to-back holding a potato between their backs. They must race from start to finish and back without dropping their potato.

From *Camp Summer Read: How to Create Your Own Summer Reading Camp* by C. Kay Gooch and Charlotte Massey.
Santa Barbara, CA: Libraries Unlimited. Copyright © 2011.

2. Forehead-to-Forehead: Campers hold the potato between their foreheads and race from start to finish without dropping their potatoes.
3. Spoon Balance: Using a kitchen serving spoon, campers must balance a potato from starting line to finish line, then transfer the potato to the next runner. The first lane of campers to finish wins.
4. Potato Fencing: Each camper gets two kitchen serving spoons and one potato. Pairing up, campers "fence" each other. While balancing a potato on one spoon, they try to use their empty spoon to knock their opponent's potato from their spoon.

Wiki Information

Mr. Potato Head website; game of "how fast can you peel a potato"

Packet Information

Potato Word Search, MonkeybarJrTV; Mr. Potato Head activity pages, Readers' Advisory Page

Book Planning Form

Title: *Crossing Bok Chitto: A Choctaw Tale of Friendship and Freedom*
ISBN-13: 978-0-938317-77-7
Author: Tim Tingle
Illustrator: Jeanne Rorex Bridges

> **Synopsis:** In the 1800s, a Choctaw girl becomes friends with a slave boy from a plantation across the great river, and when she learns that his family is in trouble, she helps them cross to freedom.

> **Interesting facts to talk about:** The Trail of Tears; the fact that it is unusual to read things about both slaves and Native Americans in the same story, Indians of the Mississippi River region, historical fiction, dream catchers

Activity 1

<u>Dream Catchers:</u> According to legend, the Native Americans used dream catchers, which hung near a person's bed and were used to catch all dreams, good or bad. The bad dreams would get caught up in the webbing and be held there until first morning light, then they burned off. The good dreams were caught, and knowing their way to the opening in the center, they would filter down into the feathers and be held there, only to return another night, to be dreamed.

Purchase Dream Catcher kits from Oriental Trading Company (http://www. orientaltrading.com). They have popsicle stick frames with leather stringing holding a nameplate in the middle. You can also create a traditional dream catcher with round hoops with crochet-thread stringing through the middle. You can add beads and feathers to the string for decorations. Another way to make a cute dream catcher can be found at PBSkids: http://pbskids.org/zoom/activities/do/dreamcatcher.html.

Snack: Indian Fry Bread

Using canned biscuits, tear each biscuit into four pieces. Drop in very hot oil until cooked brown. Serve with cinnamon sugar and honey.

Activity 2

<u>Learn about the "Trail of Tears":</u> Working in teams of two to three campers, answer questions about a picture of the Trail of Tears picture and personal accounts.

From *Camp Summer Read: How to Create Your Own Summer Reading Camp* by C. Kay Gooch and Charlotte Massey. Santa Barbara, CA: Libraries Unlimited. Copyright © 2011.

The PBS website has information about the Trail of Tears. Robert Lindneux painted the picture, the *Trail of Tears*, in 1942 (www.pbs.org/wgbh/aia/part4/4h1567.html). The Trail of Tears Observation Sheet includes the following questions:

1. What do you see? Be specific.

2. Who is in the picture? What are they doing?

3. Describe the expressions on their faces. What do they seem to be feeling?

4. Besides the Cherokees, whom else do you see in the picture? Why do you think they are in the picture?

5. Based on what you see and know, why is it called the Trail of Tears?

The Sequoya Research Center has a list of Personal Accounts from the Trail of Tears (go to www.anpa.ualr.edu/digital_library/indianvoices/family_stories/family_stories.htm). Give each team of campers a printout of a personal account of the Trail of Tears. Include the following questions on the Personal Accounts of the Trail of Tears worksheet:

1. Who did you read about?

2. Describe this person's experiences. What did he or she see and hear?

3. How did the person feel? How did it affect this person?

4. Based on what you read, discuss with your group how you would react, feel, and respond if you were forced to move from your home and walk a "Trail of Tears."

Wiki Information

Trail of Tears National Historic Trail (U.S. National Park Service): http://www.nps.gov/trte/index.htm

The Legend of the Dream Catcher: http://www.raskys.com/dreamcather.html

Packet Information

Tribes Word Search, Plains Indians Crossword, Picture Writing (page of Tribal pictures to make stories), How many words can you make from the letters in "Dream Catcher"?

Book Planning Form

Title: *What You Never Knew about Beds, Bedrooms, and Pajamas*
ISBN-13: 978-0-689-85211-4
Author: Patricia Lauber
Illustrator: John Manders

Synopsis: Presents facts on where people have slept and what they have slept on and in throughout history, covering such settings as the Stone Age, ancient Egypt, ancient Greece and Rome, and medieval Europe.

Interesting facts to talk about: *Special Note Home: The day before doing this book, send home the following note with campers:

Dear Campers:

We will be reading the book *What You Never Knew about Beds, Bedrooms, and Pajamas* tomorrow. Please feel free to wear your favorite pajamas. Also, bring any bedtime equipment you want (stuffed animal, pillow, blanket, etc.) and a flashlight for a special activity.

Nighty Night,

Ms. Gooch and Mrs. Massey

Activity 1

Pillow Cases: Each camper gets a pillowcase to personalize and paint. Make pillowcases out of the cheapest white cotton fabric you can find. The pillowcases are the same size as a travel pillow, 10 x 16 inches. On the edge of the pillowcase where the pillow goes in, write with fabric pens "Camp Summer Read – 20xx." Have a variety of fabric pens and paints for the campers to decorate their cases. Use sponges cut out in different shapes to be dipped in paint as well as paint brushes. You can purchase fabric acrylic paint and paint pens at the craft stores.

Snack: S'mores

Using a store-bought S'more maker, roast marshmallows on an electric grill that is sold for roasting marshmallows. Each camper gets one large graham cracker (to be broken in half), one roasted marshmallow, and half a Hershey bar. Sandwich all these things together, and you have a yummy snack that will make everyone want "s'more"!

Activity 2

Flashlight Tag: Turn off all the light in the library. If your area is completely dark, you need to have a little light coming in somewhere. Purchase cheap flashlights at a discount store to have extra on hand for the campers who forget to bring theirs. Each camper gets a flashlight. They then run around the library trying to tag each other with their lights. Once a person has been tagged, he or she must sit out until rescued. Another camper touching him on the head can rescue an "out" person. The play continues until only one camper is standing. The campers then make up their own variations of the game, such as they can only play in the fiction section of the library, there are two "teams" competing against each other, or they can duck but not crawl through the library. The fact that they get to turn off all the lights in the library and RUN is the majority of the excitement!

Wiki Information

Playing House Design Game: http://www.dressupgames.com/playing-house

Little Miss Matched Fun Site: http://www.missmatchedfun.com/room_decor.php

Packet Information

Sleeping Adage Alphabet Code (EnchantedLearning), quilt coloring pages (a variety of quilt square patterns with the names of the square and a little of its history; these can be found many places—use a search engine on the Internet to find resources); A Bedroom in Spanish activity page (an example of one of the items we found by searching the Internet)

Book Planning Form

Title: *George Crum and the Saratoga Chip*
ISBN-13: 978-1-58430-255-1
Author: Gaylia Taylor
Illustrator: Frank Morrison

Synopsis: Describes chef George Crum's childhood as a part Native American, part African American boy in rural 1830s New York, his adventures cooking at Moon's Lake House restaurant in Sarasota Springs, and his accidental invention of one of America's most beloved snacks.

Interesting facts to talk about: The Vanderbilts, the Adirondacks, Saratoga Springs

Activity 1

Potato Stamping: Each camper gets two halves of a potato and a plastic knife. With the first half, the camper cuts a design in the potato to use as a decorative stamp. Each table has a few paper plates of acrylic or poster paint. The campers put some paint on their potato stamps and make decorative pictures. The campers can share their stamps if they want.

With the second half of the potato, the campers cut thin potato slices to make potato chips for snack. They try as much as they can to cut the slices very thin. It is difficult with a plastic knife, so if you feel comfortable with it, you can give the campers a variety of potato peelers. There are many styles of peelers. It is a good to have a variety to let them see which one works the best!

Snack: Homemade Potato Chips

The basic recipe for potato chips is very hot oil and very thin potato slices. The campers bring you their slices, and you put them in the oil. The campers like to see their own slices cook, but make sure they stand back from the oil. You can have some very thin slices that you have cut to make sure you have some potato chips that turn out thin and crispy.

Activity 2

Research African American inventors and Create an Information Portrait: In your daily Wiki, put a link for databases to go to for the research of each inventor. Each camper chooses an African American inventor and goes to the databases to find information on that person. The camper then fills out a form with pertinent information; date of birth, place of birth, one interesting fact from childhood (if they can find it), education, most noted invention, special circumstances for invention, date of invention, any other inventions, one interesting fact from adulthood (if they can find it), and date and place of death, if applicable.

Our list of African American inventors and their inventions:

- Benjamin Banneker: clock

- Dr. Patricia E. Bath: method of eye surgery

- Bessie Blount: device for amputees to feed themselves

- Otis Boykin: electronic control devices

- Charles Brooks: street sweeper truck

- Charles Richard Drew: street mailbox

- Lloyd Augustus Hall: food preservation process

- Lonnie G. Johnson: water gun (super soaker)

- Lewis Latimer: carbon filament for lightbulbs

- Elijah McCoy: train oil cup

- Fredrick McKinley Jones: refrigeration

- Jan Ernst Matzeliger: shoe-making machine

- Garrett Morgan: gas mask

- Rufus Stokes: air purification device

- Madam C. J. Walker: hair-growing lotion

- George Washington Carver: peanut products

- Granville T. Woods: communication system

Wiki Information

Pringles potato chip can crafts: http://www.artistshelpingchildren.org/pringlespotatochipcanscraftsideaskids.html

Potato chip history: http://www.ideafinder.com/history/inventions/potatochips.htm

How potato chips are made YouTube video: http://www.youtube.com/watch?v=00cKkJGOjNU

Potato chip reviews: http://www.taquitos.net/snack_reviews/Potato_Chips

Packet Information

WordSearch; potato facts; invention planning page

Book Planning Form

Title: *Ballet of the Elephants*
ISBN-13: 978-1-59643-075-4
Author: Leda Schubert
Website: www.ledaschubert.com
Illustrator: Robert Andrew Parker

Synopsis: Tells the story of how circus owner John Ringling North, choreographer George Balanchine, and composer Igor Stravinsky teamed up to create the *Circus Polka,* a ballet for fifty elephants and fifty dancers, and describes the opening night performance in 1942.

Interesting facts to talk about: Stravinsky, circus, circus animals, Ringling Brothers

Activity 1

Ballet Puppets: Make elephant puppets from a cute coloring-page elephant. Decorate with watercolors, markers, jewels, googly eyes, and colored tulle for the tutu. Glue (or staple) them to large tongue depressors. When all the campers are finished, they can divide into three or four groups and choreograph a ballet to Circus Polka.

Alternate Puppet: Use an empty toilet paper roll for the body and glue all the elephant parts on the toilet paper roll. Have preprinted elephant parts for the students to decorate and cut out. See www.dltk-kids.com for a cute puppet.

Snack

Animal crackers and popcorn in cute red and white bags.

Activity 2

Paint Like an Elephant: Discuss humane treatment of circus elephants. Compare 1942 and now. Briefly read *Elephants Can Paint, Too!* by Katya Arnold. Discuss the organization that raises money to encourage the humane treatment of elephants. Show pictures in the book and on the Internet of the elephants painting pictures, and talk about how they are sold to raise funds for elephants' rights.

Painting: On an outside hallway, tape regular copier paper on the wall. This is your "canvas." In two-person teams, one person is the elephant, and one is the trainer. (Each person will get to play each role.) Using the commands learned from the book and Internet site, the "trainer" tells the elephant how to paint. *Up, down, across, circle, squiggle,* and *dab* are the commands. The "elephant" holds the paintbrush in one hand, which is extended out to pretend it is a trunk. The "elephant" follows the trainer's commands. Use heavy-duty art paintbrushes, not the flimsy watercolor brushes. Have many cups of poster paint available for the elephants to use and cups of water for rinsing the brushes. When everyone has had a turn to paint like an elephant, lay the paintings out to dry. When dry, write on the bottom corner, Camp Summer Read 20XX, and have the elephants sign their paintings. Mount the pictures in mat board frames you have purchased at the craft store. You will have to have the "elephant" tell you which side of the painting is the top.

Wiki Information

Ringling Bros. Circus; painting elephants

Elephant stories: http://www.elephantcountryweb.com/Elliestories.html

Elephant weight-lifting game: http://kids.nationalgeographic.com/kids/games/actiongames/geogames-elephant-weightlifting

Elephant puzzle: http://lightupyourbrain.com/flashpuzl/elephantpuzl/elephant-jigsaw-puzzle.html

Elephant foot game: http://www.onlinegames.net/games/1049/elephant-foot.html

Packet Information

Elephant Scavenger Hunt: Elephant Conservation (www.ringling.com). Questions for the page:

1. Why was the Ringling Bros. & Barnum & Bailey Center for Elephant Conservation founded?

2. Where is it located?

3. How many elephants have been born at the Elephant Conservation?

4. When was the most recent calf born?

5. What is its name?

6. What determines whether an elephant will join the circus?

7. List three ways Ringling Bros. takes care of its animals.

8. How many Asian elephants are there in the world today?

9. Take a virtual tour of the facility!

Elephant quiz comparing African and Asian elephants; Elephant Crossword; Elephant word search; Elephant dot-to-dot

Book Planning Form

Title: *Pompeii: Lost & Found*
ISBN-13: 978-0-375-82889-8
Author: Mary Pope Osborne
Author Interview about this book: http://www.randomhouse.com/teachers/catalog/display.pperl?isbn=9780375828898&view=tg
Illustrator: Frescoes by Bonnie Christensen

Synopsis: Presents a short, illustrated narrative of the city of Pompeii before the A.D. 79 eruption of Mount Vesuvius buried the city and describes how, in 1763, the city was rediscovered.

Interesting facts to talk about: Volcanoes, archeology, ancient Rome, Fresco paintings, extinct cities

Activity 1

<u>Archeology Dig and Plaster Chipping:</u> We purchase "treasures" such as rings and gold coins from Oriental Trading. The junior counselors bury them in our sand volleyball pit. The campers use rakes, shovels, and hand gardening tools to dig out the treasures as if they were archeologists. We also put one or two of the treasures in small Dixie cups filled with plaster of Paris. The campers used hammers to separate their "rocks" and paintbrushes to clean off their finds.

Snack

Bakery bread torn into chunks with olive oil to dip; string cheese

Activity 2

<u>Create a Fresco:</u> Each camper gets a piece of sturdy corrugated cardboard measuring about 9 x 12 inches, a cup of watered-down plaster of Paris (about the consistency of oatmeal), and a paintbrush (cheap brushes used to paint furniture, $1 at hardware stores). The campers "paint" the cardboard with the plaster. They can make it bumpy if they wish or create a design. This dries fairly quickly. Have campers wash out their brushes and get a color or two to paint their frescos. The campers paint their plastered boards with their big paintbrushes or little watercolor brushes. Big broad sweeping strokes, circular motions, and dabs make a beautiful painting!

From *Camp Summer Read: How to Create Your Own Summer Reading Camp* by C. Kay Gooch and Charlotte Massey. Santa Barbara, CA: Libraries Unlimited. Copyright © 2011.

Wiki Information

Make a volcano: http://kids.discovery.com/games/pompeii/pompeii.html

Explore Pompeii: http://www.rome.mrdonn.org/pompeii.html

Discovery Channel on Pompeii: http://dsc.discovery.com/convergence/pompeii/pompeii.html

Volcano photos and stories: http://www.volcanoes.com

Volcano interactive: http://www.learner.org/interactives/volcanoes

FEMA on volcanoes: http://www.fema.gov/kids/volcano.htm

Volcano quiz: http://kids.nationalgeographic.com/kids/games/puzzlesquizzes/quizyournoodle-volcanoes

Scholastic's Volcano Lab: http://www.scholastic.com/play/prevolcano.htm

Packet Information

Volcano information pages; fresco painting information; ancient Roman maps

Book Planning Form

Title: *The Greatest Skating Race: A World War II Story from the Netherlands*
ISBN-13: 978-0-689-84502-4
Author: Louise Borden
Website: http://louiseborden.com/index2.html
Illustrator: Niki Daly

> **Synopsis:** During World War II in the Netherlands, a ten-year-old boy's dream of skating in a famous race allows him to help two children escape to Belgium by ice-skating past German soldiers and other enemies.

> **Interesting facts to talk about:** World War II, Poland, ice skating (especially long distances), how old a child has to be to go somewhere without parents or other adults, escaping from somewhere or something

Activity 1

Exploring Maps of Europe: Have the campers follow the route taken in the book on a map of Europe. Then have them find their home on a U.S. map and figure out what would be about the same distance to travel. Where would they wind up? How would they get there? The children in the book skated; what could the campers do? What is the landscape between home and their final destination?

Snack

Ice cream sandwiches.

Activity 2

World War II Timeline and PowerPoint: First, the campers watch a PowerPoint presentation about the events that led to WWII, the major events of the war, and the end of the war. (These are elementary students, so surface information is fine; great detail isn't necessary.)

The campers (in teams of two or three) then get a large sheet of butcher paper (4 to 5 feet) and some pages with pictures and dates of the major events of WWII. They make a timeline cutting out the pictures and events. They may work horizontally or vertically. After they are finished, campers go look at all the other timelines and share among themselves.

From *Camp Summer Read: How to Create Your Own Summer Reading Camp* by C. Kay Gooch and Charlotte Massey.
Santa Barbara, CA: Libraries Unlimited. Copyright © 2011.

Wiki Information

Author site: http://louiseborden.com/index2.html

WWII timeline: http://www.historyplace.com/worldwar2/timeline/ww2time.htm#1939%20

History of WWII: http://www.historycentral.com/WW2/index.html

Ice-skating games: http://www.miniclip.com/games/thin-ice/en

Figure skating game: http://www.candystand.com/play/figure-skating

WWII photos: http://www.archives.gov/research/ww2/photos

Packet Information

World War II information; ice-skating coloring pages; word search

Book Planning Form

Title: *Outside and Inside Mummies*
ISBN-13: 978-0-8027-8967-9
Author: Sandra Markle
Author interview: http://christchurchcitylibraries.com/Kids/ChildrensAuthors/SandraMarkle.asp
Illustrator: Sandra Markle
Synopsis: Describes the technology used to uncover the many secrets of mummies, including how they died and their age, as well as the diet of the ancient Egyptians.
Interesting facts to talk about: Mummies, Egypt, kings and pharaohs

Activity 1

Mummy Wrap Races/Egyptian Collar and Cuffs: Divide the campers into two groups. Each does one of the activities, and then half way through, the groups switch.

Mummy Wrapping: Instead of using an exorbitant amount of toilet paper, we cut scrap fabric into 4-inch-wide strips and sew them together to make 35 yards of fabric. The original intent was to have races to see who could wrap each other the fastest. What ended up happening was that the campers had a blast wrapping each other, both with the "mummy" standing still and turning in circles!

Egyptian Collars and Cuffs: In the Oriental Trading catalog, we found Egyptian pharaoh collars and cuffs. You could also make these yourself. The campers colored them with markers and decorated them with "jewels." These collars and cuffs are used in Activity 2.

Snack

Mummy cookies or fruit roll-ups.

Activity 2

Mummy Millionaire: Watch the Steve Martin short of "King Tut." Put on the collar and cuff and perform the King Tut dance. Have the words to the song up so everyone can see them and sing along.

Wiki Information

Author interview: http://christchurchcitylibraries.com/Kids/ChildrensAuthors/SandraMarkle.asp

From *Camp Summer Read: How to Create Your Own Summer Reading Camp* by C. Kay Gooch and Charlotte Massey. Santa Barbara, CA: Libraries Unlimited. Copyright © 2011.

Ancient Egypt: Science and Technology: http://www.mos.org/quest/teaching.php%20

Make a fish mummy: http://www.exploratorium.edu/bodies/webcast_activity.html

Mummy Xpedition: http://www.nationalgeographic.com/xpeditions/activities/17/mummies.html

Mummy maker game: http://www.bbc.co.uk/history/ancient/egyptians/launch_gms_mummy_maker.shtml

Packet Information

Mummy crossword, mummy word search, words to Steve Martin's "King Tut" song

Book Planning Form

Title: *Marvelous Mattie: How Margaret E. Knight Became an Inventor*
ISBN-13: 978-0-374-34810-6
Author: Emily Arnold McCully
Illustrator: Emily Arnold McCully

Synopsis: Describes inventor Margaret E. Knight's childhood, explaining how her interest in mechanical innovations began, and tells the story of her invention of a paper-bag maker and her legal battle for the patent after someone stole her idea.

Interesting facts to talk about: Paper bags (stand-up, flat), women inventors, biographies

Activity 1

Paper-Bag Scrapbooks: These paper-bag scrapbooks are cute interactive albums to make and are great "brag" books or special gifts or keepsakes. Each camper can decide the topic of his or her scrapbook. Here are some suggestions:

favorite song, food, game, subject, book, color, movie, animal; All About Me—family, pets, favorite things, hobbies, awards. Each camper starts with two lunch-size paper bags. The tables are supplied with staplers (you might want to have a heavy-duty stapler on hand), markers, scrapbook paper, stickers, etc.

Step-by-Step Instructions:

1. Lay two (or more) paper bags together, alternating ends.

2. Fold the bags in half, and you have a "spine."

3. Staple the spines together.

4. Cover the front, back and binding with scrap-booking papers, either full sheets, collage, or a variety.

There are a lot of hiding spots for journaling tags or extra pictures in your book. Each open end of the bag can be used as a pocket where you can slide tags or pictures. What once was the bottom flap of the bag now serves as a hidden journaling feature. Use it either as a lift-the-flap type of feature where you hide journaling, or open it by cutting a slit along the fold line, and insert a tag (narrow tags work best).

Special note: Paper bags are not acid-free, meaning that over time, they will break down much faster than acid-free papers. They are also not as sturdy as a card-stock album. Use only duplicate pictures in your albums. Precious, one-of-a-kind photos and mementos should be copied or duplicated.

From *Camp Summer Read: How to Create Your Own Summer Reading Camp* by C. Kay Gooch and Charlotte Massey. Santa Barbara, CA: Libraries Unlimited. Copyright © 2011.

Snack

Popcorn in brown paper bags.

Activity 2

<u>Paper versus Plastic:</u> We did a PowerPoint presentation about "Paper vs. Plastic." This caused a lot of conversation and passionate discussion. At the end of the presentation, we gave campers a third option: reusable bags. At the time we did this activity, reusable bags were just becoming common. We gave each camper a bright neon reusable bag, and they decorated them with stick-on foam cutouts and fabric paint. If we were to do it today, we would ask the local grocery store to donate enough bags.

Wiki Information

Inventors and Inventions: http://www.42explore2.com/invent.htm

Imagination Place: http://cct2.edc.org/imagination_place

Paper-Bag Ideas: http://www.ehow.com/brown-paper-bag

Packet Information

Women in history—brainstorming web; Young Inventor Worksheet—a page to brainstorm an idea and turn it into an invention.

Book Planning Form

Title: *Comets, Stars, the Moon, and Mars: Space Poems and Paintings*
ISBN-13: 978-0-15-205372-7
Author: Douglas Florian
Illustrator: Douglas Florian

Synopsis: A collection of twenty whimsical poems about comets, the stars, the moon, and the planets.

Interesting facts to talk about: Douglas Florian books—poetry about one topic

Activity 1

Space Necklace: Premade wooden cutout space shapes (rocket, Saturn, generic planets, stars) and beads to string on yarn. Let the campers decorate the wooden pieces with glitter glue, but be sure to tell them moderation is best! Let them dry, then string them on colored yarn with wooden beads in between each piece.

Snack: Moon Balls

2 cups peanut butter

1 ⅓ cups honey

2 cups raisins

2 cups dry milk

3 ½ cups graham cracker crumbs (keep ½ cup separate)

Mix dry milk, raisins, and 3 cups graham cracker crumbs. Add honey and peanut butter, and mix well. Use your hands to mix; it works the best. Roll into small balls. Place remaining ½ cup of graham cracker crumbs in a large plastic bag. Place several balls at a time into the bag and shake, then place on a cookie sheet. Chill and eat!

Activity 2

Topic Poetry Books: Make each camper a booklet to write his or her poems. Each camper will choose a topic about which to write all their poems. The cover of the booklet

From *Camp Summer Read: How to Create Your Own Summer Reading Camp* by C. Kay Gooch and Charlotte Massey. Santa Barbara, CA: Libraries Unlimited. Copyright © 2011.

should have a place for their book title and an author byline. Always put down on the front or in the bottom middle of the back cover "Camp Summer Read 20XX." Inside the booklet, the left page will have a type of poetry with an example. The right page (facing the left example) will be a line for their title and a place for their poem. They can decorate each page after they finish their poems.

The poems we used are as follows:

- Free verse: Free verse is an irregular form of poetry in which the content is free of traditional rules.

- Acrostic: Acrostic poetry is when the first letter of each line spells a word, usually the same words as in the title.

- Cinquain: A cinquain is a short, usually unrhymed poem consisting of 22 syllables distributed as 2, 4, 6, 8, 2 in five lines.

  - Line 1: Noun

  - Line 2: Description of noun

  - Line 3: Action

  - Line 4: Feeling or effect

  - Line 5: Synonym of the initial noun

- Diamante: A diamante poem is diamond-shaped poem that use nouns, adjectives, and gerunds to describe either one central topic or two opposing topics.

  - Line 1: Noun or subject

  - Line 2: Two adjectives describing first noun

  - Line 3: Three "ing" words describing the first noun

  - Line 4: Four words: two about first noun, two about antonym or synonym

  - Line 5: Three 'ing' words about antonym or synonym

  - Line 6: Two adjectives describing antonym or synonym

  - Line 7: Antonym or synonym of Line 1

- Tanka: Tanka is a classic form of Japanese poetry (related to Haiku). It has five unrhymed lines of 5, 7, 5, 7, 7 syllables.

Wiki Information

About the sun: http://imagine.gsfc.nasa.gov/docs/science/know_l1/sun.html

Apollo 11 Interactive: http://wechoosethemoon.org

Space puzzles: http://www.crpuzzles.com/space/index.html

Space animations: http://www.tietronix.com/CreativeServices/ExamplePages/CSSpaceAnimationsAssembly.html

Your weight on another planet: http://www.solarviews.com/eng/edu/weight.htm

Models of planet sizes of planets and other space-related features: http://suzyred.com/space_models.html

Space games: http://resources.kaboose.com/games/space.html

Packet Information

The solar system vocabulary activity; crossword; solar system information page

Book Planning Form

Title: *Martina the Beautiful Cockroach: A Cuban Folktale*
ISBN-13: 978-1-56145-399-3
Author: Carmen Agra Deedy
Illustrator: Michael Austin

> **Synopsis:** A humorous retelling of a Cuban folktale in which a cockroach interviews her suitors to decide whom to marry.

> **Interesting facts to talk about:** How the same folktales are told in different cultures; cockroaches; Cuba

Activity 1

Maracas: First, put on some Cuban music!
Each camper gets an empty paper towel holder and an - 8 ½ x 11-inch piece of paper. The paper is marked so that when it is rolled around the outside of the cardboard paper towel holder, you can tell what will eventually be covered up. The campers decorate their papers and glue them around their paper-towel holders. The junior counselors will help with the next step, which is adding a little sound to the maracas. With a glue gun, glue a square of tissue paper to one end of the maraca. Next, add some dried beans and rice. Let the campers decide how much of each they want according to the sounds they make. Let the campers play their maracas to the Latin music playing.

Snack: Sopapilla with Honey

Take canned biscuits; tear each biscuit into four pieces. Drop in very hot oil until cooked brown. Serve with honey.

Activity 2

Salsa Dancing and Conga Line: Download some salsa songs from iTunes or other music sites. There are many children's versions that are appropriate and adorable! Watch a video on the Internet about how to salsa dance (do this ahead of time so you already know how). Then everyone lines up and salsas together. After you have salsaed for a while, grab your maracas and conga around the library. Some of the boys may grumble at this at first, but when it comes to the conga line, they love it. We have even had boys go home and tell their parents how much fun this was!

From *Camp Summer Read: How to Create Your Own Summer Reading Camp* by C. Kay Gooch and Charlotte Massey. Santa Barbara, CA: Libraries Unlimited. Copyright © 2011.

Wiki Information

Cootie Game: http://activegamez.com/games/1204/cootie.html

Yucky Roach World: http://yucky.discovery.com/noflash/roaches

Wikipedia: http://en.wikipedia.org/wiki/American_cockroach

Cockroach Info: http://www.cockroach-pictures.com/cockroach_facts.htm

Author's site: http://www.carmendeedy.com

Map of the Caribbean: http://www.worldatlas.com/webimage/countrys/carib.htm

Martina's site: http://www.beautifulmartina.com

United States Folklore: http://www.americanfolklore.net/ss.html

Multicultural Education: http://www.coedu.usf.edu/culture/Story/Story_Cuba_girl.htm

Pest World: http://www.pestworldforkids.org/index.html

Packet Information

American Cockroach Question Page, to be used with the Wikipedia site; map of the Caribbean

Book Planning Form

Title: *Help Me, Mr. Mutt!: Expert Answers for Dogs with People Problems*
ISBN-13: 978-0-15-204628-6
Author: Janet Stevens and Susan Stevens Crummel
Illustrator: Janet Stevens

> **Synopsis:** Dogs across the United States write to Mr. Mutt, a people expert, for help with their humans.

> **Interesting facts to talk about:** Dear Abby and other advice columns; zip codes

Activity 1

Pet Place Mat: Campers are told to bring pictures of their pet(s) ahead of time. If a camper does not have a pet, he or she can substitute a friend or relative's pet or bring a picture of a favorite "stuffed pet." The day of the activity, campers are given an 11 x 17-inch piece of paper. Campers then glue the picture to the mat and choose from an array of scrapbooking paper and stickers to decorate it. Campers may also use markers to draw pictures on their mat. The mats are laminated and given to the campers to take home and use with their pets. Their pets now have their very own pet-food/water-bowl place mat!

Snack: Puppy Chow

This is one of the most popular snacks we make. It has to fit in at least once a year!

½ cup peanut butter

¼ cup butter

1 cup chocolate chips

½ teaspoon vanilla

9 cups Crispix or Chex cereal (any flavor)

1½ cups powdered sugar

Instructions:

1. Combine peanut butter, butter, and chocolate chips in a microwave safe bowl.

2. Microwave for one minute, then stir to blend all ingredients thoroughly. Add 1/2 teaspoon vanilla. Stir well.

3. Place the 9 cups of Crispix or Chex cereal in a very large bowl.

4. Pour the peanut butter and chocolate mixture over the cereal and toss evenly, making sure all the cereal gets a good coating.

5. Coat with powdered sugar, sprinkling evenly over the cereal and tossing as you sprinkle to cover each piece well.

This is so yummy!

Activity 2

Design Stationery and Write Letter: Campers receive a lesson on how to write a letter that is delivered through the U.S. Postal Service. Campers are told ahead of time to bring their home address and an address of a friend or relative. Each camper receives a piece of writing paper with lines (www.dltk-kids.com). Use the paper that leaves an empty space in the upper right hand corner. This corner is where each camper personalizes the stationery. Ideas include drawing a fancy initial or a picture, pasting a favorite picture, or creating your own logo or coat of arms. Campers write a letter to the person they have chosen. You may have to give them ideas about what to write. Step by step, the campers are walked through addressing their envelopes and where to put the stamp they are given. Mail the campers' letters. At the end of camp we write them a letter about how much fun we had at camp so they get their own letter in the mail.

Wiki Information

Mutt Maker: http://animal.discovery.com/pet-planet/mutt-maker.html

Breed a Dog: http://pbskids.org/dragonfly/games/game_dogbreeding.html

Author's Site: http://www.susanstevenscrummel.com/ and http://www.janetstevens.com/

Packet Information

Canine crossword; American Kennel Club Hidden Picture; how to draw a dog in steps

Book Planning Form

Title: *Yum! Mmmm! Que Rico!: Americas' Sproutings*
ISBN-13: 978-1-58430-271-1
Author: Pat Mora
Website: http://www.patmora.com
YouTube author interview: http://www.youtube.com/watch?v=HObST3Jbea0
Illustrator: Rafael Lopez

> **Synopsis:** A collection of haikus that celebrates indigenous foods of the Americas, such as blueberries and vanilla, and includes information about each food's origins.

> **Interesting facts to talk about:** The difference between fruits and vegetables; haikus; jump-rope rhymes, new and old

Activity 1

Haiku Poetry Book: Campers brainstorm fruits and vegetables. These are written on strips of paper and put into a bowl. Each camper pulls out three strips, and these are the foods they use to create each haiku. The campers tear construction paper to create a picture for each food. The haiku is written on one page of the book, and the picture is glued to the other page. Foam fruit stickers are used to decorate the cover of the books.

Snack: Fruit Kabobs with Yogurt

Fruit is cut into bite-size pieces. You can use bananas, pineapple (canned or fresh), apples, grapes). Campers slide what they want onto a bamboo skewer. Campers are provided with a Dixie cup with vanilla yogurt for dipping their fruit.

Activity 2

Jump-Rope Rhymes: Jump ropes are purchased for each camper. Read through some jump-rope rhyme books and practice saying them in unison. Give all the campers their own jump ropes and let them go! Be sure to have some long ropes for group jumping. The junior counselors are great for turning the long ropes. The campers take the jump ropes home at the end of the week. In our experience, they enjoy using them all week at every break!

From *Camp Summer Read: How to Create Your Own Summer Reading Camp* by C. Kay Gooch and Charlotte Massey. Santa Barbara, CA: Libraries Unlimited. Copyright © 2011.

Wiki Information

Author website: http://www.patmora.com

Jump Rope Rhymes: http://www.gamekidsplay.net/Jump_Rope_rhymes/index.html

Create a haiku: http://www.pbs.org/parents/creativity/ideas/haiku.html

Packet Information

Symmetrical fruit pictures (finish the drawing); fruit brainstorming graphic organizer; fruit adjectives graphic organizer; jump-rope rhymes

Book Planning Form

Title: *The Luck of the Loch Ness Monster: A Tale of Picky Eating*
ISBN-13: 978-0-618-55644-1
Author: Alice Flaherty
Illustrator: Scott Magoon

Synopsis: A young American girl's picky eating habits transform a small worm into the famous Loch Ness monster.

Interesting facts to talk about: Scotland, Loch Ness monster, myths and legends; make sure you read the back flap information; share picky eater stories

Activity 1

Supertaster Experiments: Discuss what makes a supertaster, under-taster, or a regular-taster.

Supertasters experience taste with far greater intensity than the average person. About 25 percent of Americans are supertasters. Supertasters have an unusually high number of taste buds. Supertasters are more sensitive to bitter tastes and fattiness in food.

Under-tasters have a less-than-average number of taste buds. About 25 percent of Americans are under-tasters. Under-tasters may eat more because it requires more taste to satisfy them.

About 50 percent of Americans are regular-tasters.

Campers sample various types of fruits and vegetables. They then make a prediction about what kind of taster they are. Keep a graph of the predictions.

The campers then conduct the "Blue-Tongue Experiment." They wipe a swab of blue food coloring on their tongues and inspect the small circles of pink-colored tissue that polka dot their blue tongue. These are called papillae. Then, they put notebook paper reinforcement on the tongue. They can use a magnifying glass to count the little pink dots they see in the hole. (If your science lab has little handheld magnifying glasses, borrow those. We bought a set from the craft store in the party-favor section.)

If you count fewer than five dots, it means you are an under-taster. More than thirty dots indicates you are probably a supertaster. Just to be sure, campers then conduct the "Saccharin Test." Mix one packet of saccharin (Sweet'n Low) into two-thirds of a cup of water. Now campers taste the water.

The campers will probably taste a mix of both bitter and sweet but focus on which taste is stronger. If the sweet taste is dominant, it means someone is probably an under-taster. If bitter is the dominant taste, it means you are probably a supertaster. If it's a tie, you are a regular-taster.

From *Camp Summer Read: How to Create Your Own Summer Reading Camp* by C. Kay Gooch and Charlotte Massey. Santa Barbara, CA: Libraries Unlimited. Copyright © 2011.

Campers record the results and compare to their predictions.

Snack: Oatmeal cookies with Loch Ness monsters

Purchase some good-sized oatmeal cookies, vanilla frosting in a can, and Gummy Worms.

Each camper gets an oatmeal cookie, a Dixie cup of icing (you could dye it blue), a few "Nessies," and a plastic knife. The campers ice their cookies and place their "Nessies" on the top!

Activity 2

Origami Loch Ness Monsters
Have each camper bring a shoebox lid.

Go to www.ActivityVillage.co.uk for directions to fold a three-piece origami Loch Ness monster. The campers can choose from scrap-booking papers to fold their "Nessies." They can choose the same paper for all three pieces, complementing papers, or totally mismatched papers.

In the bottom of their shoebox lids, place clear-blue cellophane to simulate water. Place the origami Loch Ness monsters on the cellophane. They take some balancing, and some of the campers may want to tape theirs down.

Wiki Information

Quaker oatmeal site: http://www.quakeroats.com/home.aspx

Loch Ness site from Scotland (including live cam): http://www.lochness.com

Official Site: http://www.nessie.co.uk/index.html

Packet Information

Loch Ness coloring page; word find; supertaster experiment page

Appendix D

Sources for Packet Information

We search the Internet using various search engines to find all kinds of activities. Some of the sites we find are free, and others are fee-based. Sometimes we just get lucky with a search, as we did for the Loch Ness Origami activity, which was actually from the United Kingdom. Be diligent and keep searching, and you're sure to find what you're looking for—entertaining activities to engage your campers. The following is a list of some of the sites we use the most for activities.

Enchanted Learning: http://www.enchantedlearning.com

DLTK—Crafts for kids: http://www.dltk-kids.com

Teacher Vision: http://www.teachervision.fen.com

Child Fun: http://www.childfun.com

Have Fun Teaching: http://www.havefunteaching.com

Color Me Good: http://www.colormegood.com

Appendix E

Packet Sample: The Dog Book

The Dog Book

by Someone Special

(Insert your choice of clip art of a dog)

www.thedogbook.wikisite.com
(Insert your wiki site address for the day)

(Insert coloring page of different dog breeds)

SING WITH A FRIEND!!!!

"BINGO"

There was a farmer had a dog,

And BINGO was his name-O

B-I-N-G-O B-I-N-G-O B-I-N-G-O

And Bingo was his name-O!

Sing the song the first time through,

then on the second time replace the B in BINGO with a clap.

The third time, both the B and I are clapped instead of sung;

the fourth time B, I and N;

the fifth time B, I, N, and G and the last time,

all the letters BINGO are clapped rather than sung.

How Much Is That Doggie in the Window?

How much is that doggie in the window? (arf! arf!)

The one with the waggley tail

How much is that doggie in the window? (arf! arf!)

I do hope that doggie's for sale

(Insert dog breed word search, crossword, or other activity here)

(Insert a page about the history of dog breeds)

Appendix F

Letter to Junior Counselors

Camp Summer Read Junior Counselor Guidelines

Dear _____ ,

Thank you so much for your interest in being a Junior Counselor at Camp Summer Read this summer. So that you know what you are getting yourself into, we have outlined a few of your responsibilities. Please read over this list and let me know if there are any questions. We are looking forward to a great week–it will be so much fun!!!

Your Daily Responsibilities will be:

Make sure name tags are laid out in the morning

Have the attendance sheet out on the welcome table

Have the campers' folders stuffed with the appropriate activities for the day

Make sure the juices for snack are in the ice chest first thing in the morning

Familiarize yourself with the snack for the day and prepare the snack

Familiarize yourself with the daily activity and set out materials needed

General Guidelines:

Campers will look up to you and will want to be like you, please behave appropriately

When the teachers are giving instruction, you may listen to the discussion or prepare the snack

Make sure your conversations with other counselors are appropriate; there are lots of little ears around and they love to listen to you.

Please watch the flirting, either with each other or the campers.

This week will be an exciting time and a valuable experience for you. Volunteering for community service is a lifelong lesson you can't learn too early.

If you need a letter written to a teacher or club sponsor, please let us know and we will be more than happy to do that for you.

We are proud of you, Good Job!

Appendix G

Certificate of Participation

Camp Summer Read

HAS SUCCESSFULLY COMPLETED CAMP SUMMER READ 20XX AND HAS FULFILLED ALL REQUIREMENTS TO VOTE FOR TEXAS BLUEBONNET AWARD 20XX

_____
LIBRARIAN, GOOSE CREEK ELEMENTARY

_____
LIBRARIAN, BLANCO VERDE ELEMENTARY

Index

About the Authors

C. KAY GOOCH has a B.S. in Education and an M.L.I.S. from The University of Texas at Austin. She has been in the education field for eighteen years. She is currently the librarian at Gullett Elementary School in the same neighborhood where she grew up. Kay lives in Austin; has two grown children, Elizabeth and Edward, who have both graduated from college; and a Bassett Hound, Emmy.

CHARLOTTE MASSEY has been in the education field for twenty years. She is currently the librarian at Carpenter Hill Elementary in Buda, Texas. Charlotte lives in San Marcos, Texas, with her husband, Chris, and two children, Jackson, 10 and Ava, 3.